IN BETWEEN PLACES

IN BETWEEN PLACES

a memoir in essays **LUCY BRYAN**

HOMEBOUND PUBLICATIONS
BERKSHIRE MOUNTAINS, MASS.

HOMEBOUND PUBLICATIONS

WWW.HOMEBOUNDPUBLICATIONS.COM

Cover Design and Interior Design by Leslie M. Browning
Cover Image: © Patrimonio | A freelance illustrator from Auckland, New Zealand specializing in 1940s WPA works progress administration retro style images.
First Edition Trade Paperback 978-1-953340-52-8
(Wayfarer Books) eBook Edition 978-1-956368-21-5
(Wayfarer Books) Hardcover 978-1-956368-22-2

10 9 8 7 6 5 4 3 2 1

Homebound Publications is committed to ecological stewardship. We greatly value the natural environment and invest in environmental conservation. For each book purchased in our online store we plant one tree.

In loving memory of
Robert Lee Bryan
(1951-2012)

CONTENTS

MELT

I. VENISON

The last of the venison lies on the bottom shelf of the basement freezer below a solid lump of pastry dough and a bag of frost-bitten blueberries that never turned into a pie. The freezer could use a good cleaning. There are Tupperware containers filled with two-year-old blocks of pureed butternut squash and a long-expired loaf of bread. A sack of wheat flour rests in the back corner, near an unopened pack of bacon in a Zip-lock bag.

They're all left from before you went away—too old, too freezer burned to eat. But it's the five parcels wrapped in butcher paper that keep me from kneeling before the crowded shelves with a compost pail and a dish rag. The words you scrawled on them are runes: *Butterflies. Roast. Nicest roast. Venison trout.* I wonder if this is what widowhood feels like.

I choose the gilded fog of memory over the gloomy gospel in the freezer. Before you stilled that doe with your bullet, turned her into frozen slabs of meat, she was a breathing creature. I imagine her as a fawn, born the summer we took our vows. I see her silently crossing the slope of your parents' lawn, unaware of her own reflection in the window of your boyhood bedroom. You are no longer a boy, and this is no longer your home, but your youth wrestling trophies still cast shadows on the walls when she passes in the moonlight, wobbling on inexperienced legs. Threadbare sweatshirts and faded Levis sit in drawers, tokens of your mother's pining. The doe wades into the creek, head bent to drink, hooves wedged between the same blue rocks you piled into dams as a child, the same smooth stones I believed our one-day children would lift, hunting crawdads. How many times did you and she walk in each other's wakes before that final meeting?

You bring me home for Thanksgiving, our first shared holiday, and I am eager to enter her realm, to encounter anything as wild as I believe you are. We set out with your parents' dog, the soles of our boots trampling the tracks the doe left in yellow dust of the lane.

When the doe is three years old, a cautious mother, we move to this town and take to walking the fields of your family's farm on Wednesday evenings. You point to the tall grass where she and her fawns sleep, conjure a house with a wide porch and a dinner bell to ring in gray-eyed boys, dark curls perfumed with earth.

A year and some months later, she steps into a dark ring in the far field, a muddy circle between snowdrifts. She sniffs warm cinders, left by a bonfire you built for our friends. She senses heat on her face and winter pressing at her back, the same strange combination we felt as we stood before the flames.

There is no more talk of home-building, or of children, by the fall of her fifth year. Resentment and cruelty spring up in the fallow fields of our hearts as she grows fat on the clover your brother seeded near the orchard, above the plot we measured for a garden we never planted. Something made her careless, maybe the dizzying sweetness of the wild raspberries I planned on preserving for an infinite number of Augusts.

You shot her this time last year, early winter. I don't remember the day, if we had fought that morning, or if we had made love. It might have been a day like this one—the clouds hanging low over the valley in long, inverted mounds, like someone dragged a plow through their vapor. Or maybe it was a day like yesterday—when the sun, in its fleeting southern sweep, barely crested the comb of naked maples on the ridgetops.

She was your first kill in ten years—a decade of reading books and climbing mountains, years of living far from home. I had loved you for almost that long. I wonder if the trigger, imbued with December chill, felt familiar beneath your finger. Breathe. Aim. Squeeze. Maybe felling a deer is like riding a bicycle, peeling a potato, or kissing a lover—more reflex than intention, more muscle memory than will. No amount of time can erase that kind of learning.

For weeks her body—minus her head and entrails—hung in the barn that once housed your grandfather's dairy operation. Now, the weathered walls enclose broken farm equipment, discarded wood pallets, bales of hay. Someone driving slowly enough might have spied her through chinks in its plank walls—the silhouette of a doe, strung up by her hind legs.

When the blood had drained, your brother showed up to help you carve the meat off her bones; your father, to watch. This is what you told me: You peeled back the skin, sliced butterfly steaks off the back straps, tossed chunks of meat to be ground for burgers into a bucket. On the right flank, you noticed a strange bulge, the size of a fist. When you touched it with the tip of your knife, the blade sank in easily, and when you withdrew it, a green cascade poured out of the gash. The fluid smelled so foul that your brother—a man who can drink a case of beer in an afternoon, who shrugged about the fawn he crushed beneath his combine, who's gutted animals three times his size—ran outside and vomited. After inspecting the boil, the three of you decided it was the vestige of an old wound caused by a poorly aimed arrow or a broken branch, sharp and ill-placed. You cut away the infected flesh and brought the rest home to fill our freezer.

If I'd had a knife and a choice, I would have carved out the wounds we'd inflicted on each other and saved these things: the way the smooth, hot skin of your back felt against my cheek; our shared history—holidays with each other's families and hundreds of miles of hiking trails and wonderful classes and terrible jobs and weed entangled gardens and so many delicious meals; how neither of us had ever made love to anyone else; the way new ideas about philosophy or religion or justice could keep us talking late into the night; our wordless ritual for setting up and breaking down a campsite; the way you carried my cousin's children on your shoulders; how easy it was to make our friends feel loved, even when we couldn't make each other feel that way.

II. MORELS

What's left of the morels peek at me from the freezer compartment of my refrigerator. The bag is sandwiched between whole Roma tomatoes I froze straight from the garden and English muffins belonging to my new housemate. The chaos in that Frigidaire never fails to confound me. Just seven months ago, it was empty—white, bright, and clean. I bought it at Sears the first day I left the house without my wedding band. I haven't grown used to the unfamiliar items that show up inside it—microwaveable burritos, cheap vodka, pints of ice cream.

I am leaving. On February 16, you penned those words on an index card and left it on our coffee table. I found it on my return from the gym, after I called out your name and walked through the dark rooms of our house. Seventy-eight days later, you showed up with a grocery bag brimming with the wild mushrooms, elusive delicacies that appeared after the last snow.

We'd hunted morels the previous year, roaming the apple orchard your grandparents planted before your mother was born. After an hour of stumbling through overgrown grass, my empty bag still fluttered in the wind. But you had an eye for the near-invisible fungi. You plucked a dozen honeycombed caps from gnarled roots, and we fried them in your parents' kitchen.

This year, the conditions must have been right—warm and wet—because you collected pounds of the coveted things, brought bags of them to me and all of your friends. I took your offering as a promise, hoped that the season of melt and resurrection might restore you to me.

Alone in the kitchen after you left, I picked one up and ran my finger over the labyrinthine ridges—surprised, once again, by the firmness of something that looked so delicate and spongy. I sliced several in half, melted butter in a frying pan, cooked them soft and slick. There is a feral pleasure in their musky taste—only something uncultivated, something born of earth could thrill the tongue that way. Once I'd had my fill, I drew water into a large bowl and salted it. Then I submerged the morels and watched tiny black bugs swim out of their crevices and hollow stems.

Not all morels are perfect cones. Some are bent, hooked, or S-shaped. I aimed for symmetry as I slid a knife down their centers, one by one. Placing the congruent parts in rows on a parchment-lined baking sheet, I thought about our own strange symmetry. Could two people be more perfectly contrasting in background, in personality, in aptitudes? Even then, in your absence, I saw our opposing forces as fortuitous reciprocity.

The mushrooms arranged on that pan surprised me with their beauty. I wanted to capture their magnificence before dusting them with flour and placing them in the freezer, so I grabbed my camera and carried them outside. The afternoon sunlight fell slantwise on them, deepening the shadows in the grooves and turning their thin creases gold. I took picture after picture. Satisfied at last, I wrote *May 5* in permanent marker on two Ziplock bags and sealed the morels inside.

I'm not sure when I started eating them. I know they sat in the freezer for months.

One night in September, I brought home a friend to the bed you and I once shared. In the morning, aglow with possibility, I stole to the kitchen. I whisked eggs and milk, pushed diced onions and peppers to the edge of the cutting board. When I opened the freezer to fetch a couple of tomatoes, I saw the morels and pulled out six or seven of them. They felt airy and brittle as bird bones in my hands, and when I pressed a blade into the first, it shattered into a hundred or more fragments. I was careful to apply less force to the next.

The morels have dwindled to less than half a bag. I have eaten them in quiches, stir fry, and vegetable medleys. I've sprinkled them over homemade pizzas. I have served them to my lover over and over again, a test of will that has grown easier with time. A glimmering film of frost now coats them, but their earthy flavor remains.

I sometimes wonder what will happen when the last of them soften in my frying pan. That is the wrong question, I suppose, for the answer is obvious: I will eat them, savoring their essence as I always do. But what will it mean when they are gone? Tell me, is that a milestone to mourn, to celebrate, or to let slip away, as quietly as you did?

ON NAMING WOMEN AND MOUNTAINS

I have known these mountains before, worn the dust of these trails, sipped from these streams. A few days shy of my twenty-first birthday, I slept beside my first love in the fragrance of these evergreens. I lay next to him four years later, a wife failing in love, and watched the Milky Way bridge these jagged peaks. Five years have passed since then, and I have returned, now alone, to spend the summer in Yosemite National Park as a backpacking guide.

Here, memories make me feel like a stranger to myself. My own name scratches and constricts like an ill-fitting sweater. It comforts me to be with wild things that do not speak it. As I walk among Steller's jays and Brewer's lupine and Douglas firs, I think, you, too, wear someone else's name. This is also true of mountains, valleys, rivers, and lakes—names within names. I wonder about the people and the motivations behind these names, which I feel hesitant to say aloud.

A few days after my arrival in the park, I discover my favorite Yosemite waterfall two miles east of the backpackers' camp at Little Yosemite Valley. There, Sierra snowmelt races down a hundred-foot granite slide, an uninterrupted ribbon of white water dissolving into a broad, round pool. This basin, when viewed from above, conjures a human iris. Golden green rings the shallows, deepening into jade at the center, and stones beneath the surface reflect the sunlight in varying hues.

Wandering through a flat stretch of cedars, pines, and fir after my early morning ascent of Half Dome, I enter a canyon between the soaring walls of Moraine Dome and Bunnell Point, where the Merced River spills out of the mouth of Lost Valley. I approximate my location on my topographical map and misidentify the falls as Bunnell Cascade.

Lafayette Houghton Bunnell was many things—career soldier, surgeon, explorer, writer, historian—but foremost in my mind, he was a bestower of names. In March of 1851, at age twenty-six, he and fifty-seven other militiamen of the Mariposa Battalion became the first Whites to enter Yosemite Valley. Their commission: to capture the Yosemite tribe of the central Sierra Nevada, responsible for recent raids on mining settlements, and forcibly relocate its members to a reservation in the San Joaquin Valley.

And what to do with the newly appropriated land—with its glacial valleys, imposing rock faces, plunging waterfalls, and granite domes? As Steinbeck writes of California's early settlers in *East of Eden*, "They had to give everything they saw a name. This is the first duty of any explorer—a duty and a privilege. You must name a thing before you can note it on your hand-drawn map."

As it is with mountains, so it is with people. We name children so that they can be recognized, known, found. We give them strings of letters, a cluster of sounds by which their friends and family, their teachers and employers, and the Social Security Administration and Internal Revenue Service will identify them. We pick names that mean something. We investigate etymology, examine translations and significations. We choose the names of beloved grandparents, literary characters, historical figures, and biblical heroines. We consider possible nicknames, we sample pronunciations, and then we eliminate choices likely to garner teasing from unkind playmates. We contemplate alternate spellings and tally syllables. According to our preferences, we choose names that are modern, popular, exotic, old-fashioned, or unusual. The names must be beautiful, must delight the ears. And they must fit. As it is with mountains, so it is with people: to name is a privilege and a duty.

Lafayette Bunnell was nothing if not a man of duty. He executed his orders and, along with his fellow soldiers, assigned names—Half Dome, North Dome, Nevada Fall, Vernal Fall, the Three Brothers, Cloud's Rest.

Before Bunnell came to me by way of a misread map, I made his acquaintance in several brief, glossy histories of Yosemite National Park—the kind found in brochures and travel guides. The physician-adventurer held a certain charm for me then, as the excerpts most commonly drawn from his writings reflected a thoughtfulness uncommon among men of his time and ilk (admittedly, I have a weakness for wanderlust-afflicted intellectuals).

In his memoir, *Discovery of the Yosemite, and the Indian War of 1851, Which Led to that Event*, he gave this account: As the men of the Mariposa Battalion discussed what to call the wonderland they had "discovered," a great many names were proposed—most of them romantic, foreign, canonical, and scriptural. A number of soldiers favored "Paradise Valley." But Bunnell, according to his recounting of the conversation, suggested naming the place for its Native inhabitants. "I could not see any necessity for going to a foreign country for a name for American scenery—the grandest that had ever yet been looked upon," he wrote. "Yo-sem-i-ty… was suggestive, euphonious, and certainly American." Despite protests by several who expressed distaste at naming the valley after "vagabond murderers," Bunnell got his way.

On July 2, 1983, my parents gave me this name: Lucy Rebecca Bryan. My first name belonged to my father's maternal grandmother, my great-grandmother, Lucinda "Lucy" Collins. This is what I know of her: She was from Missouri. She earned a degree in journalism in 1912, an accomplishment I would replicate nearly a century later. Her family vacationed in Florida. That's where she met my great grandfather Harry, the younger man she married in her late twenties. She called him "Dear Boy" in the love letters my father and his siblings discovered in an attic after a family funeral. And she died when my grandmother was only sixteen. Along with her name, I inherited twelve place settings of her silver, monogrammed with the initial we both share.

Lucy means "bringer of light." When I was a child and my father was particularly enchanted with me, he would address me by this Greek translation of my name.

Rebecca is the name of my father's sister, whose red hair I've always admired. The name ornaments many branches of the Bryan family tree, back to the distant aunt who married Daniel Boone. It is an alternate spelling of Rebekah, the beautiful shepherdess of the Genesis account who married Abraham's son Isaac, endured years of barrenness, and connived to help her favored son steal his brother's blessing. This woman knew what it was to be loved, as she knew what it was to suffer. She was a complicated woman, which endears her to me.

Bryan. My father's surname. An Irish name meaning "noble." A name taken by my mother. The final in the succession of names fastened to me at birth.

After naming Yosemite Valley, Bunnell learned that the Natives living there actually called themselves the Ahwahnechee— "dwellers of the valley of the open mouth." The name Yosemite, meaning "those who kill," had been given to the region's occupants by neighboring Miwuk tribes who feared them. But Bunnell was disinclined to change the name he'd already assigned.

As Yosemite expert Daniel Anderson has pointed out, "It was common practice by European settlers… to either ignore [a Native American] place name and rename it, or, as with Yosemite, to use another Indian word for a place name."

Even so, Bunnell had a keen interest in learning the Ahwahnechee names for the Valley's features. In his memoir, he said he actively lobbied for the adoption of these names, "but this proved to be a thankless task, or at least it was an impossible one." So, he dedicated himself instead to finding suitable English sub- stitutions, often vetoing the fantastic and absurd names submitted by his companions, such as "Giant's Pillar" and "Devil's Nightcap."

Should I praise Bunnell's efforts? After all, he did preserve fragments of the language and culture of the people he had come to exile—vestiges that would otherwise have vanished. But I be- lieve that the surgeon-historian's obsession with place naming was not as innocuous as it seems.

Bunnell's memoir records his initial impression of Yosemite Valley: "Although I had suffered losses of property and friends, the natural right of the Indians to their inheritance forced itself upon my mind."

He knew. The goodness within him rose up against the Battalion's mission. What philosophical acrobatics he must have done to silence that inner voice! I believe that Bunnell's impassioned arguments for indigenous names were attempts at alleviating his guilt, that his preoccupation with those names allowed him to view himself as sympathetic to the Ahwahnechee, when in reality, he was complicit in a campaign of genocide.

I married my college sweetheart three weeks after my twenty-second birthday, and according to custom, dropped my middle name and took his surname. I have a vague recollection of penning what would become my new name, Lucy Bryan Green, on a barroom napkin sometime during my engagement—writing it over and over again in loopy cursive. The image is so silly, so absurd, that I sometimes wonder if my memory swindled it from a cheap paperback. I am certain, though, that changing my name excited me. It symbolized a transition into adulthood. It meant that I would be a wife, would build a family with the man I loved. Besides, green had always been my favorite color, and my new name made a clever email handle for a budding environmentalist: lucybgreen.

I dropped my given name without hesitation, without a second thought. A generation after the women's liberation movement, it didn't occur to me that an alternative existed. How can this be? Geography had something to do with it, I'm sure. Women (and men) of the American South have a long history of clinging tenaciously to traditions, and my religion taught me that it was my Christian duty to leave my family and join my husband's. I wanted to belong to him, to be possessed. I said as much in my vows, in which I promised to submit to his leadership. Abandoning my name came easy; surrendering my stubbornness did not.

To put your name on something, whether a woman or a mountain, signifies ownership and proclaims dominion. Few of the White explorers who flocked to the Yosemite region intended to settle there, but that doesn't mean they weren't interested in cementing their legacies and fortunes by slapping the names of their heroes, their wives and daughters, and themselves on Yosemite's most prominent and beautiful geographical features.

John Beck, an iron prospector, named Beck Lakes for himself in 1882. Homesteaders John Snyder and William Walker marked gulch, ridge, lake, and creek with their surnames. In 1909, Robert Marshall of the U.S. Geological Survey named Elizabeth Lake for his niece and Flora Lake for his cousin. He named Forsyth Peak for his close friend William Forsyth, acting superintendent of the park, and he named Mary Lake, Dorothy Lake, and Polly Dome for Forsyth's daughters. Charles Hoffmann of the Whitney Survey affixed his wife's name to May Lake, which reflects the mountain bearing his name. In 1932, Al Gardisky named Odell Lake for a "friend" and Lake Helen for a "lady friend." Park Ranger Otto M. Brown, who served as camp cook for Eleanor Roosevelt when she visited Yosemite in 1934, named Ardeth and Avonelle Lakes for his daughters. Billy Lake, Bugg Meadow, Cecile Lake, Ediza Lake, Gertrude Lake, Hart Lakes, Holcomb Lake, Laura Lake, Lily Lake, Lois Lake, Olaine Lake, Rosalie Lake, Stevenson Meadow, Sullivan Lake, Ward Lakes, Weber Lake—time has swallowed the stories of the people these places memorialize, but their names make a crowded cemetery of Yosemite maps.

In 1906, the U.S. Board on Geographic Names attempted to limit the self-interest and nepotism inherent in place-naming by implementing this policy: "Names of living persons should be applied very rarely, and only those of great eminence should be thus honored. No personal names should be attached because of relationship, friendship, or personal interest, nor should names of obscure persons be given. Names of eminent men now dead may be thus perpetuated, particularly those of early explorers, naturalists, geologists, topographers, etc."

The policy aimed to curb some of the basic human tendencies that attend the act of naming. Underlying each name is a set of values predicated on personal experience, cultural norms, and the desire for immortality. To name a place is an act of power, intrinsically self-interested.

When my husband left me after nearly six years of marriage, everyone expected me to return to Lucy Rebecca Bryan. The lawyer friend who was handling our divorce called and asked for my maiden name so he could submit the name-change forms for me. I told him I wasn't changing my name.

Why? Everyone wanted to know. *There aren't any children, thank goodness—so no need to keep the name for the sake of unity. You're still young. You were a Bryan much longer than you were a Green. Do you really want to explain to future boyfriends that you still have your ex-husband's name? Besides, why would you want to keep the name of a man who walked out on you? Don't you know how much this pains your family?*

At the time I made the decision, I'm not sure I fully understood it. In the early days, I remember thinking that I couldn't bear to wait in line at the Social Security Office and DMV. It seemed too punishing on top of all the paperwork, the meetings with the bank, the dismantling of the life we had built together. And when people asked, I told them that I'd published as Lucy Bryan Green, that I'd already established a professional identity. That sometimes shut them up.

The truth was more complicated. In my mind, Lucy Rebecca Bryan and Lucy Bryan Green represented two disparate identities. Lucy Rebecca Bryan was the girl who once argued that everything in the world was either black or white, right or wrong—self-righteous enough to think that she knew the difference. She was the teenager who sustained a series of flirtations in hopes of converting her crushes to Christianity. She held the incongruous (and equally offensive) beliefs that she deserved all the good things in her life—loving parents, a college education, thick hair, long legs, intelligence, financial stability—and that God had given them to her. It took my husband to drag me out of that box of my own making.

It was Lucy Bryan Green, not Lucy Rebecca Bryan, who learned to embrace feminism, pacifism, and non-consumerism; who dared to befriend gays and liberals and atheists. She was the one who wrote a novel, who learned to garden by trial and error, who trekked all 212 miles of the John Muir Trail. The man whose name I took played a fundamental role in me becoming that person. I didn't want to go back. I wanted to move forward.

I also wanted to take responsibility for my contributions to the mess that my marriage had become: Anger that would boil into door-slamming, hair-pulling, glass-shattering rage. My need to control everything, down to what time my husband woke up in the morning and the clothes he wore. My anxiety, which sometimes made basic tasks like doing the dishes or shopping for groceries seem insurmountable. I wanted to work on those problems as Lucy Bryan Green.

And I still liked my name. It didn't seem fair that he could take it from me. He'd already taken the canoe, a whole bookcase's worth of books (along with the bookcase), half the set of glass nesting bowls, our nicest chef's knife, two watercolors I'd painted, our cast iron patio furniture, our Honda CRV, the pine bedframe we'd stained by hand, all of the power tools, and most of the money in our bank account. Those were just the things. When he left, so did his family, many of our friends, my sense of security, the belief that I was unconditionally loved, my trust in God, my identity as a married woman, my plans to have children, and my sense of self-worth. I wouldn't let him have my name. He'd taken enough.

When I am really honest, this reality surfaces: I hoped he would change his mind, would come back. I wanted to wear his name because I still loved him.

I like the idea of having a name that has emanated from me rather than been affixed to me like a cattle brand. What if we possessed names that reflected our identities—our personality traits, our physical attributes, or the events that formed us? This practice has obvious shortcomings and limitations. Brand new babies don't have much to offer in the way of distinguishing characteristics (I'm glad not to be stuck with Won't-Sleep-Through-The-Night or Eats-Dirt); and on a practical level, surnames serve vital administrative functions.

But it has been done. A 1907 text from the Bureau of American Ethnology describes a handful of Native American naming traditions, including naming people for dreams, noteworthy events, and personal qualities. The Maidu often called infants and children nothing more than "'child,' 'baby,' or 'boy' until they were old enough to exhibit some characteristic which suggested something appropriate." In many indigenous cultures, people acquired multiple names and changed their names at "critical epochs of life" such as "birth, puberty, the first war expedition, some notable feat, elevation to chieftainship, and… retirement from active life."

I wonder if I would feel more at ease with my name if it were a recent acquisition (perhaps received on the summit of Cloud's Rest?) or if I knew I wasn't stuck with it, that it would change as often as I did.

I don't know what to do about my name. After a time of mourning and deep-dwelling pain and what felt like loss upon loss, something shifted, and I fell in love again. The man I love wants to be my husband, and I want to be his wife. So, naturally, he thinks it's time for Green to go, and I think that's perfectly reasonable. Here is an opportunity for change, but I don't like my options: I can keep my ex-husband's name, take my new husband's name, or return to my father's name. Each of those choices perpetuates a patriarchal naming system that reduces me to property (at least symbolically). None of them will leave me with a name I feel is mine.

A number of my married friends have solved this dilemma by joining their surnames in some fashion or another. That solution seems sensible, albeit clunky. But my fiancé is unwilling to drop his middle name (his father's first name) to adopt my father's surname.

I envy Cheryl Strayed, who recounts her journey on the Pacific Crest Trail in her memoir *Wild*. As she filled out her divorce papers, the surname "Strayed" came to her. She adopted it as a symbol of where she had been and what she had overcome.

I have searched my memories, maps, even the dictionary for a word that fits my identity in this fashion. For the same reasons I haven't gotten a tattoo, I don't think this possibility will work for me. I know what it is to love deeply—so deeply that you want this person near you, as close as possible, for the rest of your life. I have felt this for two men but not for a word, picture, or symbol.

"Really, would it be so bad to take my name?" my fiancé recently asked. "Don't you want to be part of my family?" The answer to the second question is easy: Yes. I love his family. The idea of joining it thrills me. But the answer to the first question isn't so straightforward. It wouldn't be a travesty to carry his name. It's an interesting name, and the old-fashioned notion of "two becoming one" still appeals to me. But I also feel an internal resistance, a need to create a protective space for myself. I want a name of my own—a name not connected to any man—because then he cannot walk out the door with it.

Yosemite and I—we're both trapped. My present name is a burden, but I have none to go to, none that would truly be mine. And Yosemite wears a misnomer given by a willing participant in our nation's oldest (and perhaps greatest) atrocity. Its landscape is littered with unfitting names. But those names will remain, and soon, I will have to choose another name.

I recently bought an updated map of Yosemite and located the waterfall I visited in the Lost Valley. It's not Bunnell Cascade, which lies further upstream at the head of the Valley. This particular cascade is marked only by a blue line and the word "Falls."

I think I will take my fiancé there when he visits me in a few weeks. We will peel off our packs and our clothes and dive into that deep green iris at the base of the falls. And it won't matter that the place has no name. Indeed, that will make it all the more wonderful.

IN BETWEEN PLACES

S ometime after we cross into West Virginia, after many miles of meandering two-lane roads, long after cell phone reception and streaming radio have vanished, my nineteen-year-old brother tells me he feels lost.

"I'm not myself anymore," Joseph says. "I just want to be my-self again."

I know what it is like to want to go back, to re-inhabit a past self from an earlier, simpler time. Recently, I saw the name of a town on a TV weather map, a town I haven't seen or thought of in over a decade. But that name—Dillwyn—opened some trap door in my mind. Out sprung a battered service station, its marquis advertising $1.36 per gallon gasoline. An acute longing filled me—a longing to be my twenty-year-old self, speeding past that station, full of blind faith in the direction she was going, the man she was heading toward. Sometimes I think it would be nice to feel that way again, to be that blithe and foolish, just for a little while.

I do not tell my brother that there is no going back, that the self he yearns for died two years ago, with our father. And I don't explain that the feelings of dissonance he's experiencing are just part of growing up. Instead I tell him that I've started meditating, that the practice of mindfulness—of dwelling in the present (or at least directing my attention there)—is helping. The losses don't feel as heavy as they used to; the longing doesn't feel so intense.

It is strange and comforting to converse with my brother like this. Twelve years my junior, Joseph was only six when I left for college, and we haven't lived within 500 miles of each other since then. The oldest and the youngest of four siblings, we're called "the bookends" by family members. But for me, the nickname also represents the years and distance between us—and our contrasting dispositions. Affable and easygoing, my brother is the foil to my high-strung, anxious personality.

In part, I've invited Joseph on this trip because I want to perpetuate the love of wilderness and adventure that our father shared with all of his children. But there are other reasons. My baby brother has always felt slightly out of reach, and I want to know him—who he is and what he thinks about and if he's okay. I want him to know me too. And walking in the woods together seems like a good way to make that happen.

We're still in the car, and already, the perennial distance has compressed. At nineteen and thirty-one, we speak as intimates. I am not sure whether to credit this change to maturity or proximity or the pain we share. Also, there are the territories we have left—his life as a college student and mine as a college professor—and the territory we have entered together—overlapping ridges of the Allegheny Mountains, fading from deep indigo to powder blue. I am experiencing the familiar inversion that occurs within me in wild places, the opening of my inner life and the internalizing of the exterior world. I'm curious if Joseph, too, feels this.

Signs for Dolly Sods Wilderness direct us down a Forest Service road unrecognized by my GPS. The screen shows us driving into a green void. Green is the right color. We travel beneath a lush canopy of summer foliage, bumping over gravel and through intermittent streams of sunlight.

Within the hour, we shoulder backpacks laden with camping equipment, rain gear, and four days' worth of summer sausage, trail mix, freeze-dried dinners, and Snickers bars. We hop from rock to rock in the sodden Blackbird Knob Trail, passing over streams, through a fern-carpeted stand of beech trees, and into the redolent shade of a red spruce grove. These are not the same giant spruces that forested the hunting grounds of the Massawomeck and Monongahela cultures centuries ago. Nor are they the ninety-foot-tall trees that German immigrant Johann Dahle drove his cattle through en route to high-altitude pastures called "sods" in the early 1800s.

This place has known loss. Loggers arrived in the late nineteenth century to hack their fortunes out of four-foot-thick trunks and enormous swathes of virgin forest. By the 1920s, the ridges and hollows had been reduced to stubble, and what little remained, fires took. Flames consumed the ancient layer of organic matter that mantled the mountain floor. The ground burned one, two, three feet deep until there was nothing more to burn, nothing left but a desolate landscape of boulders and ash.

Trees planted by the Civilian Conservation Corps in the 1930s had hardly a decade to extend their branches before World War II arrived, bringing with it more destruction. For two years, the U.S. Army used Dolly Sods as a training ground. Cabin Mountain and Blackbird Knob served as designated targets for bombs that pocked the terrain. Despite attempts to clear the area of artillery and mortar shells, signs warn present-day visitors that live bombs may lie in wait, lodged between rocks or buried beneath soil.

But we are not thinking of bombs when we turn north onto Upper Red Creek Trail. No, we are thinking of berries. For the forest has fallen away, and we have entered a vast meadow, punctuated by exposed rocks and islands of wind-stunted spruce. The name for this habitat is "heath barren," but this place is anything but barren. Blueberry and huckleberry bushes surround us, acres and acres of them. We climb, stopping periodically to fill our mouths with ripe fruit, and when we crest the hill, we see an ocean of berry bushes tumbling into swales and climbing up ridges.

The wind rushing across this land sounds like prophecy, like whispered words of the prophet Isaiah: *Beauty for ashes*.

We stop at an uprooted, sun-bleached tree. In its brittle remains, I see opportunity. We've noticed little in the way of firewood since entering this tundra, so we snap off branches and strap them to our packs.

Stirred by the transfigured landscape and by the prospect of turning lifeless limbs into heat and light, I ask Joseph, "Why do you think people are so resistant to change?"

We walk a ways, and he says, "Maybe it's just fear of losing what we have."

He is right. I'm well acquainted with attempts to capture present goodness, to convert it into a live-in diorama. I have clung, white-knuckled, to the transitory, knowing I am powerless to make it permanent. When I was twenty-two years old, I lay in bed beside my new husband, crying bitterly over words attributed to Jesus in the Gospel of Matthew: "For in the resurrection people neither marry nor are given in marriage, but are like angels in heaven." The thought that our union would not paint the skies of eternity filled me with despair.

It has been nine years since I wet my pillow with those silly, futile tears. I have learned that when you cling too tightly to any source of happiness, you either lose skin or strangle your beloved.

Joseph and I are lost. Not the existential kind of lost we spoke of in the car. And not the profound misplacement experienced by the early explorers of North America, men described by the book in my backpack as "wandering a continent about which they knew nothing...plunging into a place for which they had no words for places."

Relying on memories of a previous visit, I led us too far north, to a place without water. We had no choice but to hoist our packs onto our backs and aim for the headwaters of Red Creek, the closest water source. Then, hoping to shave half a mile off a seven-mile day, we mistook a faint footpath for a shortcut to our campsite. When it dissipated, we opted not to turn back, instead skidding down a rocky slope covered in thistles and St. John's wort.

The pond we spotted from above is no longer visible, but we've found a creek and are walking south over spongy beds of sphagnum moss. We bounce from one peaty bank to another, searching for firm footing as the stream forks and forks again. As we near the pond, rushes and reeds spring up, obscuring our view of what's ahead and slowing our progress.

"We need to get to higher ground," I say. "Let's head for the trees over there."

This proves to be no simple task. A labyrinth of streamlets winds through the shoulder-high foliage, and every few steps, the bog beneath our feet gives way, and we sink shin-deep into water. I can feel the straps of my pack digging into my shoulders, and I worry that we are destroying rare wetland plants and vernal pools, inflicting more damage on this already damaged place.

Joseph groans in frustration at his water-filled shoes. I'm frustrated too, and I feel terrible, knowing that I am the one to blame for this predicament. I curse the muck, and I am grateful when he responds with laughter. His composure in the face of the unexpected makes me think he has perspective that I lacked at his age.

I wonder if the losses my brother has experienced have made him wiser than I was at nineteen and if they have better prepared him for the losses to come. Joseph was the only one of four siblings left at home when our father received a diagnosis of stage IV prostate cancer. Daily witness to five years of slow wasting, he was barely seventeen and just a few days into his senior year of high school when our father died.

This we share: the loss of a good and gentle man who loved us fiercely. And we silently bear this grief together: that our father never reconciled himself to his imminent end. He never accepted that he would die, despite the scans showing multiplying metastases, debilitating pain in his bones, facial paralysis and warped vision, pronouncements of doctors, the arrival of hospice nurses, oxygen tubes, bedsores, and visiting clergy.

He lived for three weeks without food, one week without water—longer than anyone expected. One afternoon, at a nurse's encouragement, we surrounded his bed and told him it was okay to go. "Go where?" he rasped, indignant. Only in the depths of a morphine-assisted coma was he finally able to release, able to allow his heart the mercy of stopping.

When our father died, he left shelves of photo albums, a computer hard-drive full of digital photo files, and an entire walk-in closet lined with stacks of chronologically arranged pictures, slides, and negatives. These weren't just the traditional birthday, Christmas morning, and family vacation pictures. They featured the strange, the everyday, and the completely mundane. There are photos of us throwing temper tantrums as toddlers, of me getting my ears pierced, of my brother walking around the backyard with a BB gun. In them, we eat dinner, convalesce from colds, work on homework, sleep in front of the TV.

I now believe that my father's obsession with taking pictures was his attempt to trap the goodness of the present. Amassing a collection of moments in freeze-frame was his way of coping with the terrifying knowledge that we would grow up and he would grow old, that everything would change. Maybe he viewed his photographs as portals to the past, insurance against the losses he feared most.

They don't work that way for me. Rifling through those artifacts—two-dimensional glimpses into experiences I will never re-inhabit—makes the past, and my father, feel very far away. I prefer to imagine what life would be like if he were still here. I picture him holding my sister's daughter, who would have been his first grandchild. I imagine our family finally taking that trip out west that we always talked about, caravaning across long stretches of desert highway. Sometimes, I invent different endings. I hear him assuring me that he lived a full and satisfying life. I envision a benevolent doctor and a prescription that would have spared him those final weeks of agony. I see his lifeless lips smiling, rather than contorted by a final, ragged gasp.

I know that these fantasies are just as powerless as the piles of photographs now gathering dust in some storage space in my sister's house. I am working hard at releasing them, because I don't want to be like my father, unable to accept my reality. This is one of the reasons I've started meditating. I recognize my need for a discipline that will help me rise above the noise in my head, the relentless wingbeats of fearful, anxious, and embittered thoughts. And I hope the practice of mindfulness will give me a broader, more accurate frame of reference for my experiences and healthier ways of responding to them.

When I meditate, my aim is to remain physically still and mentally present for ten, twenty, or thirty minutes at a time. Frequently, I use physical sensation as an anchor, focusing my attention on different areas of my body. I take note of numbness, tingling, and aching, but I consciously choose not to judge those impressions as pleasant or unpleasant. Instead, I relax and let go, one part at a time.

I am not very good at this. My mind wanders frequently, and I often find myself at the end of a long chain of thoughts, minutes in the making. I respond to physical sensations automatically— repositioning, stretching, or scratching before I realize what I am doing. At the end of some sessions, I feel calm and refreshed, but just as often, I feel tired or unsatisfied. Even so, I believe that meditation is helping me. The acceptance, non-judgment, and release that I practice during these sessions are slowly becoming habits of mind, ways of engaging with my everyday experiences. What I want is to be able to interpret my father's death and manner of dying not as tragedies but simply as *what was*. When reminded of his absence, as I often am, I would like to receive it not as injustice but as *what is*. And instead of burdening myself with anxiety about the losses I will inevitably encounter—the passing of my youth, freedom, relationships, sense of identity, health, loved ones, and my time on this earth—I want to accept *what is to come* with grace. Surely, an open-handed life invites more peace than a closed-fisted one.

How fitting that the book I have chosen to carry on this trek in Dolly Sods is Rebecca Solnit's *A Field Guide to Getting Lost*. In it, she ascribes a mystical, purifying, transformative power to being lost. She invokes the words of Henry David Thoreau: "Not till we are lost, in other words, not till we have lost the world, do we begin to find ourselves, and realize where we are and the infinite extent of our relations."

This is not the kind of thinking Joseph and I were raised on. Lost was what happened to children who wandered off at the mall or county fair, who went where they weren't supposed to go and sometimes never came back. In sports and games, there were those who lost and those who won, and nobody wanted to be a loser. Our school teachers chastised us for getting lost in our thoughts. And in church, lost was the favored euphemism for the unrepentant sinner, the soul condemned to hell. It was the word the Bible used to describe people who were wicked, unclean, disobedient, and weak.

The kind of lost that we are now doesn't feel like vanishing or defeat or detachment or depravity. Though wading through this mire is exhausting, it's also gratifying. I can hear my heart and my breath. I am alive and fully engaged, connected to the earth and my brother and the act of walking.

Eventually, a muddy rut that just might be a footpath appears before us. We follow it through a cluster of alder bushes, across a grassy hummock, and into a stand of spruces. A fire ring greets us, and we whoop with delight.

On our second day in Dolly Sods, we hike along the spine of Cabin Mountain beneath roiling gray clouds. We traverse shadowy forests, hills, bogs, and long-abandoned orchards. It is early afternoon, and rain is falling steady and cold when we arrive at our campsite, a tongue of land at the intersection of the two upper branches of Red Creek. Rain soaks through my clothes to my bare skin, and soon, I'm shivering. We set up the tent, and I climb inside and change into dry clothes.

"Hey, I'm going exploring," Joseph says.

"I think I'm just going to stay here and read," I reply, slipping into my sleeping bag. "I'm still freezing."

At some point, the murmuring of the creek and irregular rhythm of raindrops falling on the tent lull me to sleep. I wake up more than an hour later to a loud crack and high-spirited cheers from a handful of young men who've set up camp nearby. The sun has come out, infusing my tent with orange light. I climb out and watch the men, bare-chested and bearded, lug an entire tree down the trail.

I look around for Joseph, but I don't see him, so I walk to the rocky peninsula at the junction of the forks. The water is lower than it was the last time I was here, quietly spilling over a semicircular ledge where the two creek branches meet. I walk upstream along rippled slabs of Pottsville sandstone, stepping over water-filled fissures and cavities and pausing to admire the pale pink rhododendron blossoms on the opposite shore. When the creek narrows and the banks become steep, I cup my hands and shout "Joseph" upstream, but my call goes unreturned.

I walk back to our camp through the woods and head up the left fork of the creek, picking my way over boulders. It's slow-going in this direction—the water has plotted a wilder course in this branch, forming a series of chutes and cascades—so after shouting Joseph's name again, I turn around and head for the trail that parallels Red Creek's downstream run.

This isn't the first time Joseph has disappeared in the wilderness. Just last night, he vanished and didn't return until after dusk, when I called for him to haul water and help with dinner. When he arrived, he told me about the beavers he'd heard slapping their tails. Then he pulled me away from the campfire to show me the cluster of ghostly white plants he'd found growing at the base of a tree.

"What are they?" he asked, kneeling to get a better look at their bent, bell-shaped heads.

"Indian pipe," I told him. I explained that the plants were non-photosynthetic, that instead of living off of sunlight, they lived off of decaying organic matter.

This is why I never chastise him for wandering off. Joseph's childlike curiosity is a quality I am trying to cultivate in myself—what Zen Buddhists call "beginner's mind," a way of experiencing the fullness and beauty of the present.

For fifteen minutes, I walk along the trail, which allows me to survey Red Creek from the steep slope above its western bank. I scan the rocky creekbed below, but I don't see Joseph. When too many trees come between me and the water, I half-walk half-slide my way to the creek's edge. Then I climb back to the trail, the poison of worry unfurling beneath my ribs. Aware of my tendency to assume the worst and overreact, I order myself to calm down. Joseph is a Boy Scout of Eagle rank, perfectly capable of handling himself in the woods. I turn toward camp, hoping he will be there when I return.

He is not.

I decide to stay busy purifying water. Sitting on a rock, swirling a UV light in liter after liter of creek water, I attempt to focus on my breathing. I attune myself to the feeling of air in my nostrils, air in my throat, air filling then leaving my lungs, and I try to let my anxious thoughts glide past like clouds. But my mind's eye centers on darkness, discounting rational explanations in favor of this image: Joseph face-down in the creek—unconscious, maybe drowned—having slipped on a rock and hit his head. I debate when to seek help from nearby campers. 5? 5:30? It's been nearly three hours since I've seen him. When is it reasonable to panic?

Reason and mindfulness do not prevail. I imagine a helicopter circling, first responders tromping down the trail with a rescue litter. I imagine my mother crumpling on the kitchen floor. In my gut, I feel the sharp, sucking sensation of fresh loss. And in that moment, my past, present, and imagined future coalesce. I am not just the negligent sister, who led her brother to his end. I am the forsaken wife, kneeling on the floor of a dark living room, reading and rereading the note on the coffee table. And I am the fatherless daughter, folded over the hospital bed in my parents' bedroom, cheek pressed against an unmoving chest. A familiar refrain loops in my head: *Come back. Come back. Come back.*

Once more, I walk to the base of the forks and shout "Joseph!" downstream. Then I issue the summons our father taught us, a call he and his college friends developed to find each other in crowds: "Cha-choo! Cha-choo!" I listen and hear only moving water and birdsong.

I repeat this process upstream, at both the upper and lower forks. Searching for movement, I see nothing but the fluid motion of the creek and trembling leaves.

Slowly, I walk back to our campsite. I look at my watch and see that it is almost 5:00. A wave of anguish swallows me, and I throw my head back and wail. My eyes blur with tears. My arms go limp. My shoulders shake. Then, like the grieving woman in the Gospel stories, I hear a voice behind me. I hear my name.

I whirl around, and there is Joseph—unharmed, smiling, whole.

He sees that I'm crying and rushes to hug me. "I heard you calling. Are you okay? What happened?"

"I thought you were dead," I say.

"Why?" he asks.

"You were gone for three hours. I didn't know where you were."

Joseph tilts his head. "Really? It was that long?"

I nod.

"Sorry," he says. Then he pulls his phone out of his pocket. "Look what I found."

On his camera roll, there are close-up pictures of a yellow amanita mushroom and a water-filled maple leaf. Bright red tips of British soldier lichen top pale green stems. There are flat stones piled into a cairn and side-by-side cross-sections of rocks split in two. There's a crawfish no bigger than a quarter, peeling curls of birch bark, and shelves of bracket fungi climbing up a tree.

"Beautiful," I say.

Later, I ponder the terror I experienced when faced with the unlikely possibility of my brother's death. What was that? The survival instinct in hyper-drive? A vestigial compulsion to protect anyone who shares my DNA? We are intelligent creatures endowed with consciousness. Maybe that's part of the problem— we "tax [our] lives with forethought of grief," as the farmer-poet Wendell Berry so aptly puts it. But the large frontal lobes of our brains also allow us to control our biological impulses and our perceptions of reality. Caution and an awareness of danger are useful attitudes, but what advantage is there to unremitting dread of death, the most inevitable and ordinary condition of existence? We cannot escape this truth: we will lose what we have— all that we love and hate, everything we know and do not know, our minds and memories and bodies. All of us will die. Given this reality, shouldn't our species be better at letting go?

I am not advocating indifference to death, and I am not suggesting that the particular, intimate losses we experience are meaningless. Poet Pattiann Rogers' thoughts on this matter resonate with me: "Every death, whether creature or flower, whether a thousand pine needles of the forest or a weak hatchling pushed from its nest or a whale stranded on a beach or a deer starving on the plains... each and every death is mighty and significant."

We are part of a great web of being, all of us connected. When one creature ceases to be, that changes the fabric of existence. What I want is to wrap myself in this ever-changing fabric—this substrate in which death and life are inextricable and incarnation is fleeting—and to feel peace. I have a long way to go, but I will continue meditating, hoping the seeds of acceptance and letting go take root.

The next morning, I spend ten minutes watching a slug inch its way over a branch we set in its path. I am reminded of two principles of mindfulness—ones I find difficult to implement and easy to ignore: patience and non-striving. I want to be a non-anxious, open, fully present person, but punishing myself for slow progress is counterproductive. Mindfulness instructor Jon Kabat-Zinn describes movement toward our goals in meditation not as linear but as an unfolding we allow to happen within ourselves. I find this reassuring.

After breakfast, we set off on a side trip to Breathed Mountain. Without weight on our backs, we move quickly, discussing the essay Joseph read last night when he borrowed my book.

"I like what she said about being lost," he says, "how you get un-lost not by going back, but by turning into something else. That makes sense."

"Instar," I say. The word has been rolling around my mind since I read its definition yesterday—*a stage between two successive molts.* "I like the idea of being a creature in the process of becoming."

I tell Joseph about a podcast I recently listened to about the metamorphosis of butterflies: A caterpillar constructs its chrysalis and, once safely inside, liquefies. Cut open that fragile shell early on, and you will find primordial goo. Given enough time, that goo will aggregate into a butterfly. How that happens is something of a mystery, even to entomologists.

What most intrigues me about the metaphor of insect meta-morphosis is that transformation hinges on inaction and undoing. Sure, the larva must build its chrysalis, but the act of building isn't the point. Pupation is where the magic happens. In trans-mutation, doing is subordinate to being.

I want to ask Joseph what and who and how he wants to be, but I'm concerned those questions will just make him feel more pressure. The burden of doing already weighs heavy on him. *Declare a major. Choose the right classes. Get that internship. Make connections and money and a name for yourself.* I want to tell him not to worry about any of that—it's all bullshit anyway, distrac-tions from the deep stuff, from the kind of living that will give him a rich inner life. But who am I to criticize worry? And why should I assume my way of making meaning is the best or only way? How to live—that's something Joseph will have to figure out for himself.

We turn off the rocky trail into an opening in a rhododendron thicket. From there, we follow a series of cairns through the forest, up a pile of boulders, and onto the summit of Breathed Mountain, which reminds me of an enormous fractured tabletop. We leap over cracks and chasms and scramble over inclined ledges, work-ing our way to the eastern edge of the escarpment. Finally, we stop and take in the view. We face the deep, narrow gorge formed by Red Creek, which marks the end of the Allegheny Plateau and the beginning of the Allegheny Front. Standing at the precipice, we stare into undulating green ridges.

It has been raining since we arrived at our campsite on the banks of Alder Run. We managed to collect a little firewood and to cover it with my poncho before it got too wet to burn, but the rain hasn't let up. Undeterred by the weather, Joseph has gone out and returned from his daily exploration. We've cooked and eaten dinner in the rain. There's nothing to do but sit in the tent and wait for night to come. We play tic-tac-toe and dots on scrap paper. We drain my phone battery listening to a reading of a short story. Neither of us feel much like talking.

I'm just starting to feel sleepy when Joseph announces that he thinks he can get a fire started on the island in the creek. He tells me that earlier, he discovered a fire ring there that's sheltered by a thick stand of spruce trees. Their overlapping branches will have kept it relatively dry.

"You don't have to come," he says.

I admit that I'm disinclined to abandon the warmth and dryness of my sleeping bag. But it is our last night in Dolly Sods, and I don't want to lose this time with Joseph. I don my jacket and pull on soggy shoes. Arms loaded with firewood, we wobble unsteadily across the creek.

It takes a while, but Joseph eventually produces a small flame. Soon, darkness swallows the forest around us. There is only the fire, and our faces, and flickering light on nearby tree trunks. We listen to water—that gentle carver of mountains—dripping through the trees, gliding over and around stones in its eternal downstream passage. We sit on this island, this in-between place—content, for the moment, to be together, to be still.

GLYPHS

We pass the rocks on the first day of our honey-
moon. We're someplace west of Nephi, Utah, careen-
ing through Salt Creek Canyon on State Road 132.
We wind through hills of sagebrush and juniper, cruise between
walls the color of storm clouds, streaked with russet veins. Then,
rounding a bend, we see a mound of boulders, their faces painted
with bright block letters. Proclamations like "TREVAN LOVES
SKYLA" and "J.B. + K.T. FOREVER" fill the driver's side window for a few seconds. I watch the patchwork of graffiti recede in
the rearview mirror.

Half an hour later, we turn onto Highway 50, "the loneliest
road in America." The Sevier Desert stretches out before us, a dull
green expanse that melts into indigo peaks at some indeterminate
point in the distance. The motor hums, and the air ahead of us
undulates with heat. Jet-lagged and doused in afternoon light, my
new husband dozes in the passenger seat.

My eyes rest on the long, straight line of asphalt ahead of me,
but my mind returns to Salt Creek Canyon. I imagine love-struck
teenagers, laughing in the cool desert night, kissing beneath stars
undiminished by city lights. I conjure rocks still radiating the heat
of day, the clink-clink-clink of a can being shaken, the sharp smell
of spray paint. Their fingers unclasp to touch the pigment, lifting
temporary souvenirs of Cherry Red and Cobalt Blue. When they

finish, they celebrate with a shared cigarette or a Bud Light—or maybe just a pack of Skittles. Then they lie in the bed of his brother's truck and trace the arc of the Milky Way, believing that it, too, belongs to them.

I could ask why they paint their names in that place, risking injury, incarceration, and the sting of regret—but I already know the answer. First love makes fanatics of us all. We inscribe words on stone and receive the work of our hands as prophecy. Each shimmering moment affirms our faith in what we imagine will be.

But what happens when the symbols we create outlive their meanings? I suspect most of those Juab County kids have already discovered the fragility of love and the ache of unmet expectations. What's it like for them, I wonder, to pass their marks with changed hearts?

In 2008, I walked into a tattoo parlor with my first husband. We were planning a trip out west to celebrate our third wedding anniversary—a month-long, 212-mile trek on the John Muir Trail. Worried about damaging or losing our wedding bands or prying them off of swollen or sprained fingers, we'd decided to leave them behind.

I don't remember who came up with the idea to emblazon each other's initials on our ring fingers. We envisioned thin lines in tattoo green on the soft flesh between palm and knuckle—an unadorned B on my finger and the right angle of an L on his. For me, it was important that people know we were married, even when we weren't wearing our rings. Being a wife gave me an identity and status. The day I wed, just weeks after my twenty-second birthday, was the day people started treating me like an adult. I also wanted to signal that I had been chosen, assessed and found worthy of lifelong companionship. And secretly—presciently, perhaps—I craved assurance that my spouse still wanted me.

I've often wondered why my ex-husband agreed to the tattoos. According to the narrative he later shared, he was already weary of me then—worn down by long-standing power struggles that erupted in daily fights, tired of pitting his desire for freedom against my need for control. He'd already begun thinking about ending our marriage, though it would take a few more years for that idea to come to fruition. Did he still have hope for us, hope that a month in the woods might plaster the cracks in our relationship? Or would the L on his hand serve as a kind of guard, a keeper of a boundary he simultaneously dreaded and fantasized about crossing?

The shop occupied a small storefront on one of the college town's main avenues. Stock pictures of butterflies, fairies, Celtic crosses, and barbed wire bands crowded its waiting room walls. We were the first arrivals of the day. The receptionist pulled aside a curtain and admitted us to a back room, where we described our vision to the tattoo artist—a balding man with an impressive salt-and-pepper beard.

"I don't do couple tattoos," he told us. "No names, no hearts, nothing like that."

"All we're asking for is a letter on each of our hands," I explained. "No one has to know what they mean."

"You will," he said. "The both of you will. And if it don't work out, you'll come crying to me."

I laughed. I wanted to tell him that we'd meant it when we vowed "until death do us part"—that even if things got hard (or harder), we'd keep that promise to each other. I really believed that. But I recognized I was dealing with a cynic.

"Don't worry—you wouldn't be the one I'd come crying to," I offered.

He shook his head.

"B is also the first letter of my maiden name—so if we split up, I could just say that's what it stands for."

"Nope."

I made a final appeal: "Don't finger tattoos fade quickly, anyway? I mean, they wouldn't actually be permanent if we didn't maintain them, right?"

"Sorry, sweetheart. Won't do it."

We left the store and stood on the sidewalk, arms crossed. A traffic light turned green and released a surge of cars. Normally, once I'd committed to a course of action, I wasn't easily deterred—but this exchange left me feeling off-kilter. There were several other tattoo shops in town, and we could have easily tried another just down the road. Instead, we climbed into our rusting station wagon and went home.

Nate and I drive west for hours, past dried-up lakes and wooden signs pointing to Death Canyon and Blind Valley, over mountain passes, through gulfs ablaze with apricot mallow. This is the Great Basin, a region of mountain chains and arid valleys that spans six states, rolling from Utah's Wasatch Range all the way to the Sierra Nevada.

Eventually, I turn onto a gravel road. Half an hour later, after crossing into Nevada and navigating miles of rocky, washed-out ruts, we arrive at Hendry's Creek Trailhead. Last week, I learned about this place from an online backpacker forum. The post described Mt. Moriah Wilderness—a 90,000-acre territory in the Snake Range—as a "wildly remote land" where we could find "solitude in large doses." This appealed to me. We wouldn't have to vie for a decent campsite. We could make love in the open. We'd have enough time and quiet to listen to each other, the birds, our own thoughts.

Standing here, cramming gear into my pack, I feel excited. But I also feel a hint of trepidation. Until this afternoon, when we finally found topographic maps at a Utah Geological Survey bookstore, we didn't know how much water we'd need to carry or how much elevation we'd gain. I'm still not sure if our trail will be maintained or marked by blazes. I don't know if there will be mosquitoes. I have no idea how cold it will get at night, though it's a scorching 97 degrees right now, according to the temperature gauge on our dust-coated rental car. We'll start in desert and ascend a canyon to a high plateau, but other than that, I have only a vague sense of the landscape we're about to enter.

We've equipped ourselves well. We've got plenty of food, layers of clothing, a compass, a med kit, and iodine pills in case our water purifier breaks. We've also got good instincts honed by experience. I believe this will be a grand adventure, but I also know that entering an isolated wilderness means accepting certain risks: We could lose our way. We could grow tired of each other's company. One or both of us could get seriously hurt. A lot like marriage.

I sign my name in the trail register and stare at it, unaccustomed to seeing Nate's surname in place of the one I've been using for the last decade—and still uneasy about my choice to adopt it.

We hoist our packs onto our backs and set off. Cicadas serenade us from the brush, crackling like kindling in the yellow light of evening.

I'd like to think that I'm better prepared for marriage this time around. I'm older, for one—more secure in myself and a hell of a lot more independent. I know how to mow a lawn, manage my finances, and live alone. I'm better about asking for help when I need it and sucking it up when I don't. My anxiety and anger aren't the problems they used to be. I meditate. I practice yoga. I actively cultivate self-awareness and an appreciation of my partner's way of being in the world. Experience has taught me to live more open-handed, to plan less, to be kinder to the people I love.

I've also shed many of the illusions I brought into my first marriage: The idea that saying "I do" mystically brings two hearts and minds into perfect alignment. The belief that having a husband means never feeling lonely. A mistaken trust in the inviolability and strength of the marital bond.

The man I wed last month is affectionate and funny and devoid of greed. He eschews politics of any kind. He makes up songs about our cat and writes riveting short stories with deeply flawed protagonists. He has Scandinavian good looks and forges beautiful kitchen knives in his father's blacksmith shop—a craft that leaves his skin smelling of steel filings and sawdust. He is a good listener and a better lover. Unswervingly honest, he has little tolerance for self-pity and manipulation. I think he will make a good husband, and I believe I can be a good partner to him too.

But our relationship has vulnerabilities: I am more ambitious than he is, more focused on my career—yet I envy his leisure time, and I think he sometimes envies my successes. I like to be comforted when I'm sick or upset, but he prefers stoicism. I enjoy socializing and meeting new people; he finds small talk tedious. My tendency toward panic irks him, and his aloofness frustrates me. Each of us possesses the capacity to deeply wound the other: I am capable of rage, and he is capable of disdain. I'm not sure we have seen each other's worst.

Two nights before our wedding, I asked Nate if he was afraid. He stared at the ceiling—thinking, maybe, or reluctant to answer.

"I'm afraid," I confessed.

"Of what?" he asked.

"I'm afraid of our differences. I'm afraid I'll become intolerable to you. What if we build a life together, and then you take it from me? I don't want to go through that again. And I don't want us to hurt each other."

Our eyes met for a moment, and he looked away. Fresh shaven, blond hair recently trimmed, he looked much younger than his thirty-three years.

"I'm afraid I'll stop loving you—that one day, I'll just be done," he said. "I mean, I don't think that will happen, but who knows?"

These were hard words to hear—words that triggered a throbbing beneath my breastbone. But they also carried a small measure of comfort. At least, years down the road, I would not find a forgotten notebook filled with his handwriting. I would not have to read the catalog of doubts he suffered about marrying me before walking down the aisle. I would not burn with shame, knowing that, reactive and self-absorbed as I'd been, it would have been difficult—maybe impossible—for him to speak truth.

I offered Nate the chance to change direction—to choose something else or someone else. He extended me the same offer. But we agreed that we had enough faith in each other, enough optimism about our union, to move forward.

I believe the candid words Nate and I exchanged bode well for our relationship. To enter a marriage without doubt seems short-sighted. But given the right conditions, misgivings can morph into justifications for bringing the house down. My hope is that doubt revealed proves less destructive than doubt concealed. I also think our fears point to healthy desires—to love each other well, to avoid inflicting misery, to protect our own hearts. But who can predict what currency doubt, hope, fear, and desire carry in the land of voluntary kinship? Sometimes it's hard to tell a signpost from a pile of stones.

On the second day of our trek, we stop to catch our breath in an aspen grove. Behind us: eight miles of trail bordered by canyon walls, thirteen or fourteen creek crossings, flooded boots. At the outset, only a cottonwood here and there for shade, gleaming quartz crystals, lizards scurrying for shelter, columns of pale pink penstemon growing on slopes. Then, a fragrant canopy of firs and ponderosa pines, blackberry thorns that snagged our clothes. All of this, an uninterrupted ascent—3,000 vertical feet, maybe more. And the day is far from done.

We prop our packs against a downed tree and fish out granola bars and beef jerky. Nate sits down to study the map, and I roam among silver trunks. Hundreds of others have stopped here, in this very grove. I read the messages they left in the smooth, pale bark of these aspens—the offspring of a root system that's probably tens of thousands of years old. I'm curious if the Forest Service employees who carved "Camp No 8 US FS 6·67" also hauled up the stove that now rusts in the grass a few yards away. The earliest imprint I find says either "Jan 1913" or "Jon 1913." The whimsical whorls on the J and n give the impression of a name rather than a month. I see poetry in the carving "Emeron / B / Aug. 4 / 1933," and when we begin hiking again, I notice dozens of other scorings by the same man.

Nate and I cross meadows, evergreen forests, and sun-dappled glades. Wherever there are aspens, there are names. I scan the engravings and listen for the whisper of leaves, like soft rain—but the clamor of the creek drowns out subtler sounds.

I wonder about the authors of these glyphs. Some of the recent additions, like "Zoe '11," were surely trekkers, like us. But who was "Sam Hall 1936"? Did he work for the Forest Service— or maybe the Civilian Conservation Corps? More likely, he was a herder, leading sheep or cattle to summer grazing grounds. Did he carve out of boredom, custom, or a need to affirm his existence? He could have been staking a claim, I suppose, but by the time he made his mark, other names already filled this forest. His is just one in the stenciled chorus that inhabits this mountain.

The nature of that chorus seems different than the rock graffiti that called out to me yesterday—not just because most of the names here stand alone, but because this place is solitary, a day's walk from a trailhead at the end of thirteen miles of unpaved road in a far-flung desert basin. I'm curious if the carvers even intended their inscriptions for passersby, given that most witnesses stare uncomprehending—black eyes beholding with the alert, inscrutable gaze of animals. Maybe they were meant for no one. Or maybe they were meant for anyone. I imagine them speaking to each other: *Let us rejoice in this secret: what it is to stand in the shadow of this mountain, to draw breath in this fierce and beautiful landscape, to sleep in the lap of a giant. May I remain in this place long after I have gone to dust.*

It occurs to me that carving one's name in a tree is an act of faith—faith that the tree will stand despite all of the forces that could bring it down: earthquake or avalanche, fire or flood, sawblade or pestilence, or changing climate.

Marrying, too, means entrusting oneself to an imperfect partner under unreliable conditions. Why, then, become a wife again? Why wed at all? For millennia, the institution of marriage has reduced (and still reduces) women to property. It has excluded (and still excludes) couples who don't conform to gender norms. It fails so many, in spite of deep love and good intentions. It traps and disillusions and dissolves with disconcerting frequency. It offers no guarantee of happiness, security, or success.

I know these truths, yet the idea of marriage still captivates me. I'm unable to surrender certain notions about what is possible when two well-matched individuals commit to a common journey. I long to know and to be known, and I believe that the comfort of companionship and the solace of shared experience may sustain us through loss and disappointment and hurt. The allure of discovering something wondrous and hitherto untasted also compels me. What is the view like from fifteen years, or fifty?

Is conceiving a child akin to building a fire—a mysterious and dangerous conversion of matter? What is our combined capacity for goodness, for strength, for creativity?

Nate would have been content to claim the substance of marriage—long-term commitment, shared responsibilities, intimacy, compromise, and enmeshed lives—without ceremony or proclamation. He made it clear that he needed no utterance of vows or signing of certificates.

But for me, symbols hold import. Rituals convey meaning. Perhaps this belief stems from my culture or my Episcopalian upbringing or something swirling in my DNA (whatever it was that made our human ancestors paint and chisel images onto cave walls and cliff faces).

I am grateful that Nate stood beside me under a century-old sycamore, surrounded by family. It feels significant that we spoke our willingness to *strive* and *make efforts* and *work toward* and *work with* (modest vows, penned with the knowledge that we will fall short, and with the hope that our center will hold). What is a wedding, if not a trail register—a declaration of intent to walk together into the unknown?

We come to a meadow where an avalanche has parted the forest. It offers a wide view of the sky and a glimpse of the blue-black shoulder of Mount Moriah. This will make a nice campsite, we decide, so we tuck our packs behind a tree and continue with only water and a few snacks. Our heavy loads slowed our progress, and we hope, unencumbered, we will move fast enough to make it to the summit. But our muscles falter, and our hearts leap into our throats. The unremitting climb and high altitude have depleted our energy.

Hendry's Creek narrows, its waters parting around moss-covered rocks and its banks adorned by winged columbine blossoms. The once-roaring run becomes a thread, then a patch of soggy ground as we cross a windswept glen beneath the south face of the mountain. We pass a gnarled tree that we think is a bristlecone pine and a trunk gouged by elk antlers. After emerging from a final stunted stand of aspens, we ascend and descend a series of bald ridges—each higher than the last, each offering a better view of the overlapping peaks to the south. Our impression of the summit changes as our approach takes us east. What once appeared as a gently sloping crest now looks steep and blanketed by snow.

My body feels unfamiliar. My feet are anvils—the blood in my veins, sludge. I stop every ten paces to gulp air. Nate could pass me, but he doesn't. We arrive together, at last, at an enormous plateau beneath the mountain's rocky pinnacle—"the Table." Eleven thousand feet above sea level, the treeless expanse stretches to the northern horizon. We walk into flatland over rock shards and hardy tufts of grass. I've read that elk and bighorn sheep graze here. Their droppings pepper the ground, and I seek out their forms in the gray-green plain before me, but I see only earth and sky. All is still, save the motion of our bodies and our clothes flapping in the wind. As we drift across the plateau, the sense that it would be easy to get lost out here, swallowed by this emptiness, unsettles me. Gradually, the mountains to the north come into view, blue swells against a blue sky.

We decide not to attempt the summit. I am exhausted. Nate's tired too. Already, our shadows fall long and thin to the east. Shivering, we layer sausage and cheese on crackers and swallow our victory meal. Then we turn our backs on an unclimbed peak, an unseen vista, an adventure forgone. I am okay with this. Our hearts still brim with the strange splendor of this place. Dinner will still satisfy, and the fire will still warm us. I can only hope that every plan we ever abandon will leave us this content.

"Should we add our names?" I ask, surveying the aspens bordering our campsite.

The idea defies my leave-no-trace philosophy, but the carvings feel as much a dimension of this place as the creek and wildflowers and stones. Though they serve no ecological purpose, I would not see them erased.

"Yes," Nate says. "I think so."

But we don't get up right then. Nate stokes the fire, and I peek into the foil pouches beside me to check whether our freeze-dried dinners have rehydrated. My mind weighs the act we intend to undertake. I feel hesitant—in part because it's vandalism, but more so because of its symbolic power. I recall the graffiti rocks in Salt Creek Canyon and the tattoo I'm glad I never got.

What if we don't make it? What happens when one of us dies? How will it feel, then, to know that our conjoined names adorn an aspen on a remote mountain in Nevada?

I decide I'm willing to find out. After dinner, we walk a few paces into the forest, and I select a thick trunk with a smooth surface.

"Hello, Cliff Bellander, 1932," I say to a neighboring tree—a genetic clone of the one we have chosen, their shared roots twined beneath our boots.

Nate unsheathes a camp knife he forged with his own hands and sinks the blade into the soft bark. Carefully, he traces lines and curves, removing slivers of wood. He offers me the knife at some point, and I carve part of the heart encompassing "Lucy + Nate 2015." When we are finished, I run my fingers over the impressions, inhaling the earthy fragrance of phloem.

Afterward, sitting beside the fire, we pass a bottle of whiskey between us.

"Someday, our children will come here and find our names," Nate says.

These words surprise me, coming from my decidedly unromantic husband, who seldom talks about his dreams for the future. The off-hand comment is lovely, though. And so is his face—soot-streaked and radiant in the firelight. And so are the pure mountain air and the song of the creek and the stars emerging in the twilight.

Beside us, the aspens abide—monuments to fleeting moments and lives lived, beings both ancient and impermanent, clinging to the earth and to each other.

CICADAS FOR LUNCH

The cicadas have barely begun emerging from their seventeen years in the dark—crawling out of the ground and bursting the confines of their exoskeletons—when my four-year-old niece walks into the kitchen with an open container of them. She stands before me—this flaxen-haired, azure-eyed fairy child—gazing into a trove of squirming, flapping bugs with an expression of utter delight.

No, it's not delight. It's something else. Wonder? Desire? Anticipation.

"We're going to eat them for lunch," she announces.

My father-in-law confirms this by firing up the stove beneath a cast-iron skillet.

I want to press pause. Or rewind. There hasn't been enough time to prepare. Nate warned me that his family ate cicadas during the last big hatch, half his lifetime ago. But I expected more ceremony. Some kind of ritual. An invitation, at least.

Yesterday, I walked up the hill beneath the telephone line and saw hundreds of their vacant, toffee-colored shells clinging to thigh-high blades of grass. The brittle husks swayed in the breeze beneath fragrant white blossoms of wild roses. Somewhere nearby, their former inhabitants peered from beady, red eyes—iridescent wings folded, as if in prayer, over the black armor of their bodies. In a week's time, the metallic din of their mating calls will make it impossible to hold conversations outside at midday.

My niece thrusts the plastic container toward me so that I can get a better look at her captives. There must be forty or fifty of them scuttling over each other, frantically attempting to scale the edges. I imagine the Tupperware slipping her grip and hitting the worn wood floor—the horde scurrying in every direction. I step backward. Then, self-conscious, I force myself to move in close. Their wings make a familiar sound—something between a hiss and a crackle.

It's the same sound from the bug cave scene in *Indiana Jones and the Temple of Doom*—the one that starts when Indy and his eleven-year-old sidekick, Short Round, enter a secret passage-way and notice crunching under their feet. Indy lights a match to reveal a writhing mat of roaches, beetles, and centipedes, then brushes a giant mantis off of his companion's leg. As an adult, I realize how ridiculous that scene is. Many of the bugs it features are neither cave-dwellers nor native to India—and their contrived confluence is one of the lesser inaccuracies in a film that peddles racist caricatures of India's peoples, places, and religions. But in the hundred or more times I watched that scene as a kid, I felt exactly what Steven Spielberg wanted me to: horror, disgust, and a hair-raising jumpiness that inclined me to slap every tickle and itch. I can't help but wonder if that movie conditioned the flight response I feel every time a stinkbug lands on me or a roach skit-ters across the kitchen floor.

My dad also deserves some credit for my insect aversion. On more than one occasion, the man caught rattlesnakes with his bare hands, but he couldn't kill a cockroach without giving himself a rousing pep talk and emitting a series of high-pitched screams. Such scenes of irrational terror unfolded frequently in our central Florida house.

The contrast does not elude me as my father-in-law empties the container of cicadas into the oiled skillet—as if they were mushrooms or sliced onions—and clamps a lid over them.

"It's just a country way of life," Nate pipes up.

Or maybe that's his voice in my head, teasing me with the refrain he's been chanting since we arrived in rural Ohio two weeks ago. We've decided to spend the summer here in this community of homesteaders, where he grew up. I'm the newest addition, and my city girl ways—my inability to wield a sledgehammer, steer a loaded wheelbarrow, or feed the chickens without letting one escape—have been a reliable source of comedy.

But I want to belong to this family and this place. I yearned for that before Nate was my husband, or my lover, or even my friend. We were just classmates in a writing workshop when I read one of his stories and felt a profound longing for the home he'd described—or something like it. And here I am, in that home, watching my artist father-in-law sprinkle salt and brewer's yeast over sizzling cicadas. Most of them are belly up, their bright orange legs and wing joints faded to brown. He picks one out of the pan and pops it in his mouth. Then he pours a few into a hand-painted porcelain bowl, which he gives to my niece. She begins casually munching them, like potato chips.

Someone offers me one, and I hold it in my hand, reminding myself that people all over the world subsist on bugs—that they're sustainable, self-propagating sources of protein.

"I don't want to," I plead. But I do, sort of.

My niece is watching me. I think of the showgirl Kate Capshaw played in Indiana Jones—how ridiculous she seemed as she shrieked her way through the bug cave to save Indy and Short Round from a booby trap. No one's life depends on me eating a cicada, but I do worry about transferring my squeamishness to my niece, about contaminating her openness and curiosity with fear.

I decide to count out loud, like I used to before jumping into cold water as a kid. Everyone joins in, and we say "three" in unison. Then I open my mouth and toss the cicada inside.

DIRTY HANDS

We've logged more than fifteen hours on the road when we finally cross the Florida-Georgia line. The van stops on the shoulder of a two-lane highway, and we spill onto the berm—nine college students and me, the faculty "learning partner" on this environmental service trip. After stretching our backs and shaking out our legs, we snap a group selfie in front of a big, blue sign that says, "Welcome to FLORIDA: THE SUNSHINE STATE." A smaller sign with the words "Governor Rick Scott" hangs beneath it.

I haven't yet heard the news released this morning by the Florida Center for Investigative Reporting: Since 2011, Gov. Rick Scott has been subjecting state employees to an unwritten ban on the terms "global warming" and "climate change." At this point, I know little about the state politics that directly oppose the work I've signed up to do this week, even though I'm a native Floridian. And even though eight generations of my family have lived and died on this subtropical peninsula, I know next to nothing about the place we're headed to—a nature preserve 50 miles west of Tallahassee.

But the students know this: They live in a world that humans have polluted, exploited, and marred. And they want to help. They're propelled by youthful energy and an earnest desire to undo the damage our species has done. So instead of partying on white beaches an hour south of our destination, they've committed spring break to eating vegetarian meals, living on a poverty line budget, turning off their cellphones, sleeping in tents, and planting wiregrass seeds for The Nature Conservancy.

As for me, I'm not convinced that we can repair what we've destroyed. And I'm skeptical of human meddling, even well-intentioned efforts to preserve what's left of wild places. Although I look forward to learning about an endangered ecosystem, I doubt that the work we do this week will have any meaningful environmental impact. In fact, I feel conflicted about our mission. Sure, we'll leave with a deeper appreciation of the beauty and complexity of our planet. But is that worth burning through more than one hundred gallons of gasoline on a 1,600-mile road trip? Is it worth introducing bug spray, sunscreen, and micro-trash to the place we're trying to help? And might participating in a hands-on, management-heavy approach to conservation unintentionally make us complicit in the destruction we're seeking to remedy?

We drive into Apalachicola Bluffs and Ravines Preserve on a dirt road. My first impression of the place is that it looks disturbed. Spindly pines, cacti, oak shrubs, and tufts of dry grass jut of out of an endless expanse of pale orange sand. I'm not sure whether this is a landscape of hardy survivors or foolhardy settlers, but it seems to be recovering from a terrible trauma. I am right, in a sense. In the mid-1900s, timber and paper companies clear-cut, windrowed, and established slash pine plantations on much of this preserve, wiping out the native ecosystem. But what I'm seeing now is much closer to indigenous habitat than what was here half a century ago.

The students and I set up tents and hammocks in an oak grove near staff houses and a garage with a couple of open-air shower stalls built on back. Brown anoles scurry into the brush as we walk down the road to the preserve's education center, where we cook a dinner of veggie fajitas and enjoy the sunset from a picnic table on the back patio.

Long ago, before the arrival of European settlers, these sandhills were part of an open canopy of longleaf pine and native grasses that spanned the southern coastal plain. Maintained by periodic wildfires, Florida's longleaf savannahs became some of the most biologically rich regions in the temperate zone. Scientists have documented more than forty plant species per square meter in the remnants of these communities, which historically provided habitat for gopher tortoises, red cockaded woodpeckers, and Florida panthers—all currently listed as endangered species.

But the lightning-ignited fires that once swept across northern Florida at regular intervals no longer burn. Fire suppression policies and manmade barriers, such as roads, have allowed hardwoods to dominate and transform the landscape. Less than 5 percent remains of the 90-million-acre longleaf savannah that once stretched from Virginia to Florida to Texas, nearly unbroken.

In the morning, we return to the education center for an orientation led by Brian Pelc, the natural area restoration specialist who coordinated our visit. He tells us The Nature Conservancy acquired the 6,295 acres that would become Apalachicola Bluffs and Ravines Preserve in 1982. Its work here over the last three decades is part of a large-scale, long-term project aimed at growing the longleaf pine ecosystem to 8 million acres by 2024.

Brian explains that The Nature Conservancy's goal is to "save the whole ecosystem." It's the kind of mission the students are eager to dedicate themselves to—the kind of mission that can fuel the monotonous and backbreaking work of planting wiregrass seeds for hours and days on end.

According to Brian, saving the longleaf pine ecosystem isn't a matter of raising fences and letting nature take its course. "You can't slap a lock on [the preserve] and walk away," he explains. "Property needs to be managed. What we figured out is that we needed fire."

We get a vivid representation of this principle when he tows us through the preserve on a trailer. At one point, he stops and directs our attention to one side of the road—a restoration site that Conservancy staff burned about a year ago. We peer into a golden sea of wiregrass, interspersed with gently swaying longleaf pines. Then we survey the gray grass and crowded shrubs on the other side of the road, an area awaiting controlled burn.

It doesn't take an expert to identify the healthier ecological community. But I also see human interference everywhere I look. I see it in the skeletons of oversized oaks—selected for slow demise via chainsaw "girdling." I see it in the diesel-fueled tractors used to seed wiregrass into bare sand and the bright blue tanks of biocide used to exterminate unwanted and nonnative species. I see it in invasive species themselves. When Brian identifies a swath of cogon grass, cordoned off by pink flagging tape, I think: *Who but the restorers could have introduced that menace so deep in the preserve? Surely it arrived in the grooves of a tire or the tread of a boot.*

That evening, the students and I sit on oak stumps around the fire pit in our campsite and discuss what we've observed. This place doesn't conform to our conceptions of wilderness. It's not uncontrolled, untouched, untrammeled. It's not, as wilderness historian Roderick Nash has put it, "a self-willed land."

"Maybe this isn't wilderness," I suggest. I point out that even if the native ecosystem is restored, it won't be self-sustaining. It will need humans because it needs fire. This thought depresses me. If I had to hinge my survival on the unwavering dedication of a single species, I wouldn't pick humans.

At 8 a.m. Tuesday morning, we report to the on-site nursery. Its tables are lined with nearly 2,000 plastic seeding trays—each with ninety-six empty cells. Brian explains that our goal is to plant as many wiregrass seeds as possible over the next three days. The plugs that grow in these cells will be planted by hand in areas that tractors can't reach.

Soon, I fall into a rhythm: Haul soil in a five-gallon bucket, and dump it over a tray. Tamp the soil into the cells with a wooden peg. Pour more soil over the tray. Tamp again. Place a pinch of wiregrass seeds into each cell. Spread a thin layer of soil over the seeds. Wipe the plastic borders between the cells. Repeat.

The simplicity of this cycle leaves my mind free to consider questions of scale. This week, our group will provide 240 hours of labor. If we plant 100,000 wiregrass seeds, and 75,000 of them germinate—that's enough to cover roughly fifteen acres with one plant every square yard. That's just .2 percent of this preserve, which is a mere .08 percent of The Nature Conservancy's 2024 restoration goal (assuming every planted plug survives). It's hard to imagine this being enough, and it's easy to imagine it being too much.

Still, I enjoy the tactility of the work—the steaming soil mix, its coarseness and heft, and the wispy near-weightlessness of wiregrass seeds. Planting feels good, and a longing for it to be good rises within me. I want to be persuaded that our efforts (and the broader efforts they fall under) are helping this place.

That evening, we take a hike with a resident botanist. We walk down a dirt road and dip into one of the preserve's steephead ravines—extraordinary geological features that drew The Nature Conservancy to this site.

A network of underground rivers flows 150 feet beneath these sandhills, which were once the floor of an ancient ocean. And for several million years, springs seeping from the hidden waterways have carved deep, narrow gullies in the sand. During the last ice age, plant and animal species took refuge in the temperate forests this place provided. Many of them remained in the steephead ravines after the glaciers retreated, creating rare and remarkable ecosystems.

As we descend a sharp slope, the air grows cool and damp. We seem to have stumbled into an Appalachian mountain hollow. Mountain laurel, beech trees, and white oak grow amidst cypress trees and loblolly pines. We come to a clear stream at the base of the ravine and remove our shoes. For half an hour, we wade upstream alongside salamanders and crawfish, and later, we return to the banks to avoid a water moccasin. We also stop to examine the red blooms of a Florida anise tree and the delicate branches of a Florida yew. These "glacial stragglers" never returned north when the ice age ended and can only be found in this region.

The walk gives me the opportunity to talk to Damian Smith, a member of the preserve's restoration crew. I ask him why he thinks all this work—decades of human effort poured into this tiny speck of a place—matters.

"We're preserving natural history," he says, explaining that without such endeavors, this record of the past—and the rare species contained within it—might be lost forever.

I pose the same question to Brian the next day as we plant seeds together. He tells me that this project is doing more than creating a living exhibit; the preserve is also directly benefiting humans by creating clean air, clean water, and places to recreate. It may also have an important role to play as the effects of global climate change unfold, he says, since biodiverse habitats are better equipped to handle losses and changes than sparser ecosystems.

"But how do you weigh the benefits of intervention against unknown risks?" I ask. "How do you know there won't be some unintended and terrible consequence?"

Brian's answer is practical: The team here uses a combination of expertise and instinct to make decisions—and they test interventions on a small scale before applying them broadly. The strategies that now enable the preserve's crew to restore 200 acres of ground cover per year have been honed and proven over time.

We put wiregrass planting on hold when a load of 700 longleaf pine plugs arrives—overflow from a nearby state park. The plugs need to get in the ground quickly, so we encircle the bed of a pick-up truck to receive instructions. Then we scatter across several acres of healthy wiregrass, shoulders saddled with canvas bags. I think of the reusable bags I take to the grocery store—symbols of my desire to live in harmony with the earth, but also reminders of the gross inadequacy of my individual efforts. Hauling these pines feels far more satisfying. I sink a hole digger into the sand, palm the warm, damp weight of a root ball, and gently press it into the ground. These motions reverberate with meaning: I am giving life to something—not just a tree, but to hundreds of other beings that will depend on this tree for their survival. I look at my dirty hands and feel a conversion taking place, a web of cracks splitting my brittle shell of cynicism.

Deeply engaging with this place, listening to people who know it and love it well, sleeping on a particular patch of earth and feeling it on my fingertips and lips and in between my toes has given me hope. Maybe it is within our reach to save whole ecosystems. And maybe we make that happen by doing small things (like planting seeds) that are part of small undertakings (like restoring an acre) that are part of bigger initiatives (like managing a preserve) that are part of big movements (like reestablishing 8 million acres of longleaf pine savannah).

I think of something one of my group's student leaders said earlier this week: "I don't see [wilderness] as a separate thing... I see us more as a part of it."

Those words struck me as naive then, but I receive them as wisdom now. In this act of planting a longleaf pine, I am neither an interloper, meddling with what I do not understand, nor a doctor, imposing an alien cure on my helpless patient. Rather, I am part of a complex ecosystem that is slowly healing itself, an ecosystem that includes humans (for the moment, at least).

The final night of our trip, David Printiss, The Nature Conservancy's North Florida Conservation Director, treats us to a barbeque in his front lawn, just up the hill from the nursery where we've seeded 130,000 wiregrass plugs.

After the meal, I ask David how he staves off pessimism when confronted with setbacks like Gov. Scott's ban on the term "climate change."

He shrugs and reminds me of what they've been able to accomplish in spite of political and systemic challenges: The Nature Conservancy has pioneered groundcover restoration for the longleaf pine ecosystem—uncharted territory when the site was purchased three decades ago. And what they've learned hasn't just enabled them to reclaim thousands of acres here—it's opened up partnerships and exchanges with publicly owned lands, like the neighboring Torreya State Park and Apalachicola National Forest.

The problem they're wrestling with now, David says, is recruiting people to the field of land management. There's work to be done, but there aren't enough applicants for the available jobs.

Tomorrow, we will drive back to Virginia, soil still caked beneath our fingernails, and I don't know what will happen next. I don't know how many of the seeds we planted will survive long enough to spread fire across these sandhills. I don't know if any of these students will choose to make environmental restoration their life's work. I don't know what the carbon in our atmosphere will do to this preserve or to us or to this planet.

Contemplating the tract of restored habitat in front of me, I look for the wasteland I surveyed five days ago, but I cannot find it. Evening gilds the wiregrass, florets nodding over anthills and gopher tortoise mounds. Birds and toads and crickets sing mightily. Longleaf pines stand at attention, branches adorned with green tassels that conceal silver, heat-deflecting buds. On the horizon to the southeast, the treetops dip low, marking the mouth of a steephead ravine, a portal to an ancient world.

Far-off laughter rises from the backyard, where the students are taking turns on a swing, sailing feet-first over the Apalachicola River basin. I close my eyes, inhale air laced with the scent of approaching rain, and turn to join them.

THE WEIGHT
AND WONDER OF
EVERYTHING WE DO
NOT KNOW

I'm not sure how to respond when the pastor of the Mennonite church I've attended for the last two years invites me, over email, to become an official member of the congregation. What am I supposed to say—that I'm not sure whether I belong in church at all? That I feel incredibly uncertain about the things I'm supposed to believe as a Christian (for instance, that Jesus resurrected from the dead or that there's an afterlife)? That what I do believe would have gotten me excommunicated or burned at the stake for much of church history?

The thing is, I like and trust this pastor, despite my instinctive skepticism of people in power. On Sundays, she preaches impassioned sermons about bridging cultural, economic, and political divides. She's not afraid to grapple with the Bible's contradictions, its misogyny, or its brutality. She doesn't wear makeup or own a car. Like me, she's in a profession historically occupied (and still dominated) by men. Like me, she's a woman over the age of thirty without children. I suspect she knows what it's like to feel like an outsider or a misfit—to defy expectations simply by being what she is. So, I decide to take a risk and ask her if we can discuss church membership in person.

We meet at a local coffee shop, where I tell her, "I may be a bit of a strange case."

I explain that I grew up in the church, that as a teenager and young adult, I had a strong faith, a devout practice, and what I perceived as a "personal relationship" with Jesus. But over the last decade, I've become increasingly less certain. Many days, I think it probable that there is no God, no divine presence, no grand design—that any meaning in life is meaning I make. But then sometimes—when I'm in the woods or staring into the starry depths of the night sky or singing a hymn in church—I feel this warmth, this sense of communion with everything in existence, and I think, "Maybe there is something out there."

My pastor asks if I know what prompted this change.

I mention the handful of events that have spawned my questions: In my early twenties, I caught a Christian in a position of authority stealing, then endured his threats and verbal abuse for more than a year. The husband I supported through divinity school divorced me and left the faith. I watched my father die an excruciating death; religion did little to alleviate his physical agony or his existential dread. And the deeper I got into my education, the more intellectual hang-ups I developed. I've come to see Christianity and its holy book as products of particular historical, political, and social contexts. I've developed a nuanced morality and conception of justice that sometimes clash with church doctrines. And my fascination with science has made it hard to believe in a spiritual realm for which there is no empirical evidence.

I tell my pastor, too, why I still show up to church on Sundays: Because I find the stories of the Bible powerful and revelatory, even if they're just stories. Because I think it's valuable to set aside a couple of hours every week to consider how to bring justice, love, and healing into our world. Because I want to be part of a community of people who sing together and eat together and share each other's joys and burdens. Because if there's any possibility that The Divine exists, I want to inhabit spaces where I might encounter it.

"So do you feel a yearning to have your faith restored?" my pastor asks.

"I don't know," I answer. I explain that I don't really want to be the person I was when I unquestioningly believed, but that I do occasionally miss the sense of control that prayer gave me, as well as that feeling of being intimately known and unconditionally loved by God. Mostly, I try to accept not knowing. "Maybe I'm more Buddhist than Christian, these days," I joke.

She nods, and something in her expression (a glimmer of recognition?) makes me think she might tell me I'm not alone, that there are others like me in our congregation. Instead, she praises my lack of anger, remarking that many people feel angry when they lose their faith or retreat from God *because* they're angry. She adds that my willingness to show up strikes her as an act of faith. God has a responsibility to show up too, she says.

Neither of us revives the topic of church membership. I won't be able to make the public profession of belief required of all members—that much is clear. We exchange warm goodbyes, expressions of gratitude for an honest conversation. But I feel familiar questions hovering in the pauses between our words: *Are there others like me? Is there a name for what I am? Why am I this way?*

The old stories tell us that we were made in the image of a God who delineated light from darkness, earth from sky, sea from land, woman from man—a God who granted people the privilege of naming all living things. The new stories tell us that we descend from creatures who could find patterns in disorder—a trait that enabled them to predict outcomes, distinguish threats, and live long enough to produce offspring with the same ability to impose order on chaos. Both narratives remind me that it's human nature to categorize, to define, to name.

So what do we call a person whose religious experience is characterized by profound uncertainty? Believer or unbeliever? Saint or sinner? Saved or lost? Agnostic? Quasi-spiritual? Confused?

What concerns me is not restoring my faith to its former luster (or even protecting what's left of it) but whether my abiding uncertainty indicates some kind of pathology. Despite my attempts to accept my spiritual state, I sometimes worry that my inability to embrace belief or disbelief indicates psychological weakness or willful self-deception. I could be clinging to religion, against all reason, because I don't want to face the alternative: That none of this really matters. That love and kindness and cruelty and pain don't have any broader significance. That oblivion awaits us all.

Or what if God is real, and some kind of spiritual infirmity prevents me from seeing it? It's possible that I'm heedless as the ancient Israelites, who according to Hebrew scripture, stubbornly refused to trust God and believe his prophets—even after navigating the parted waters of the Red Sea in their flight from Egypt, even after dining on manna from heaven, even after receiving divine retribution for their disobedience via exile, enslavement, and death. In general, the Bible looks unfavorably upon the uncertain.

The Epistle of James warned the early Christians: "The one who doubts is like a wave of the sea, driven and tossed by the wind; for the doubter, being double-minded and unstable in every way, must not expect to receive anything from the Lord." And though I avoid the evangelical circles I inhabited as a teenager, words uttered in that time still haunt me: "So, because you are lukewarm, and neither cold nor hot, I am about to spit you out of my mouth." Over and over again, I heard preachers invoke this verse from the Book of Revelation to discourage doubt and questioning—to suggest that the territory between belief and unbelief is an unholy wilderness.

Yet here I am, a body suspended between two planets. And despite feeling pressure to choose—to join the inhabitants of one or the other—I just can't. Although I long for the belonging and stability that choice would provide, part of me likes it here in the middle, where I am free to observe both spheres, to skim both skies as I feel inclined. But is it possible to build a home here? Can I find the meaning, community, and identity I seek in this space between worlds?

It only recently occurred to me to look to science for answers to my questions—an astonishing lapse, given that I teach college students how to plan, propose, and write about scientific inquiry projects. Perhaps this oversight is a consequence of my history. During the last decade, as my religious convictions faltered, my interest in evolutionary theory, ecology, and cosmology intensified—and naturally (albeit unscientifically), I assumed a causal relationship between these trends. It didn't help that graduate school threw me into a sea of intelligent, accomplished people, many of whom thought that science and religion offer incompatible ways of interpreting reality. More than once, I saw classmates berated for bringing up their religious convictions, and I quickly learned to compartmentalize my religious and academic identities.

But last summer, I encountered an interview with Robin Wall Kimmerer, a botanist and member of the Citizen Potawatomi Nation, on the relationship between scientific and indigenous ways of knowing. She suggested that disparate knowledge systems have the potential to illuminate and inform each other. The point is not blending, she said, but symbiosis, which leaves both systems intact as they work toward common purposes.

I began wondering how the part of me that values scientific, empirical knowledge might converse with the part of me that is drawn to church on Sundays, the part that senses sacredness in the universe. Could they work toward the common purpose of helping me come to terms with what I am? Was symbiosis even possible?

I've decided to delve into my questions the same way I instruct my students to delve into theirs: Go to the literature. Get lost in scientific texts and journals. Search for threads and themes and gaps and contradictions. Discover whether your questions have been answered, or how they might be answered, or whether they're worth asking at all.

Are there others like me?

In my late teens and early twenties, my Christian friends routinely talked about their religious questions and doubts. All around me, young people were interrogating the beliefs they'd been brought up with, attempting to define their own values and identities. But over the years, I've seen my peers veer in one direction or the other—either becoming more confident in their beliefs or abandoning organized religion altogether (a growing trend in America, especially among my generation). I can count on one hand the number of older adults I've encountered who admit profound religious uncertainty and still actively participate in religious communities.

Data from large-scale, long-term sociological studies confirm my impression that Americans tend to become surer of their religious beliefs as they age. And notably, the majority of adults in every age group (even young adults) express absolute certainty in the existence of God or a universal spirit—63 percent of Americans, overall, according to the Pew Research Center's 2014 Religious Landscape Survey (RLS). While uncertainty is far less common, it is a documented phenomenon. About 2 percent of 2014 RLS respondents said they don't know if they believe in God or a universal spirit, and another 5 percent said they believe but are "not too certain" or "not at all certain."

If the RLS accurately represents America, then among people who attend religious services weekly, approximately 2 percent are unsure about the existence of God. So in my church, on any given Sunday, there might be four or five of us in the congregation— though I suspect more, given my church's openness to people like me. I'm also far more likely to encounter my kind at work than I previously suspected. According to a study published in 2009, about one in five professors identifies as believing in God some of the time or believing in God with doubts.

These studies have revealed to me that wherever I am, there are probably kindred spirits nearby—people who are seeking The Divine, despite intense uncertainty. Maybe our shadows have overlapped as we've passed each other on campus. Maybe we've re-treated to the same mountain trails, immersed in thought. Maybe our alto and soprano have intertwined at the back of our church. Maybe the same books or articles or scientific studies have set our synapses ablaze. I take comfort in knowing this: the middle is not a void.

Is there a name for what I am?

Yes, it turns out. Social psychologist Daniel Batson coined a term for my spiritual state seven years before I was born. In 1976, he published an article in the *Journal for the Scientific Study of Religion* that introduced a "quest orientation" toward religion. Batson's predecessors had theorized that church-goers' attitudes toward religion fall on an intrinsic-to-extrinsic continuum. For those with intrinsic orientations, religion was a "master-motive" and an ultimate source of significance, while for those with ex-trinsic orientations, religion was utilitarian—a means to solace, security, status, or community. But Batson found a group of peo-ple who didn't fit this continuum: those who "view religion as an endless process of probing and questioning generated by the tensions, contradictions, and tragedies in their own lives and in society." For these people, religion was not necessarily a means or an end but a quest.

When surveyed, individuals with quest orientations tend to affirm the following claims, among others:

> 1. I have been driven to ask religious questions out of a growing awareness of the tensions in my world and in my relation to my world.

2. My life experiences have led me to rethink my religious convictions.

3. As I grow and change, I expect my religion also to grow and change.

4. I am constantly questioning my religious beliefs.

5. It might be said that I value my religious doubts and uncertainties.

Together, those declarations form a brief spiritual biography of the last decade of my life.

I like the term quest orientation. The word "quest" evokes the archetypal journeys that populate literature. As a human on a quest, I join the ranks of Odysseus, Beowulf, Janie Crawford, even Jesus. And the word "orientation" implies a perspective or direction, rather than a disorder or diagnosis.

Indeed, much of the research on quest orientation over the last three decades has revealed its merits. Studies have shown that questers display more complexity of thought about existential concerns than their intrinsic and extrinsic counterparts. They're better at integrating alternative perspectives into their worldviews and at critically evaluating their own beliefs. They tend to have low levels of prejudice and high regard for equality and fairness. One study of Christian college students found that quest orientation coincides with a triad of personality traits. First, questers are highly empathetic. Secondly, they exhibit "androgynous social sensitivity"—which means that they don't confine themselves to stereotypically "masculine" or "feminine" behaviors and are comfortable being "assertive, emotionally expressive, competitive, yielding, affectionate, and independent." Finally, questers show disregard for making a good impression. They prefer "real and genuine" conversations and resist social conventions that might incline them to conceal their opinions or misrepresent themselves.

These findings come as a huge relief. Not only do they give me a name, but they also assure me that there is goodness in this wilderness. It would seem that the fruits of questing are self-awareness, compassion, and authenticity—and as Jesus said in the Gospel of Matthew, "A good tree cannot bear bad fruit, nor can a bad tree bear good fruit." I am reassured, too, by research that has distinguished quest orientation from agnosticism—the belief that nothing can be known about the nature or existence of God. Over the last couple of years, I've often identified as agnostic, for lack of a better descriptor. But the term never felt quite right. It seemed to suggest passive resignation, a shrug, a lack of interest in religion and spirituality. I prefer "quest orientation" because it suggests action and intention.

It's fitting that the word quest derives from the Latin verb *quaerere*—to seek, to inquire. I think I've been wrong about my uncertainty. Many times, I've thought of myself as an exile, relegated to an outer darkness where the voice of God cannot be heard and the face of God cannot be seen. But I now recognize that I haven't been cast out of certainty—rather, I've been drawn into mystery.

Why am I this way?

People are complex—shaped by their genetics, social contexts, personal experiences, natural environments, and desires. I have no illusions that I could trace the labyrinthine lineage of my quest orientation, but I want to understand its roots to whatever extent I'm able.

If social scientists are right, the part of me that gravitates to religion may be attributable, in some measure, to gender and geography. Women are more likely than men to believe in God, and they pray, read scripture, and attend religious services more often than men. As a Southerner, I come from the most religious region of the country (in my experience, southerners assume you're a Christian until you prove otherwise).

On the other hand, scientific evidence confirms my suspicion that my education and profession have contributed to my religious doubts. Although the majority of my fellow academics profess belief in God or a higher power, higher levels of education are associated with a more critical view of religion, and atheism and agnosticism occur at significantly higher rates among college and university professors than in the general population.

It's probable that my personal tragedies have also precipitated doubt and uncertainty. Sociologist Darren Sherkat has argued that experiences of "struggle, torment, and suffering" may promote doubt in divine beings, causing people to "question the existence of a God that would allow human suffering."

He's right. The "voice of God" that I heard (or imagined hearing) in my younger years went silent the night my first husband left me. And as cancer slowly consumed my father's organs and bones, I watched angrily as visiting clergy prayed for a miraculous healing. In the darkness, I made a humbler plea: *Take him. Kyrie, eleison. Christe, eleison.* And to think, those hardships are but a drop in the sea of suffering that covers this planet and inundates human and natural history! I've yet to encounter a theology that adequately accounts for all of this anguish.

Psychologists have posited that certain personality traits and cognitive styles drive belief and disbelief. What research has revealed about these characteristics underscores my sense of in-between-ness. While believers tend to value tradition, security, and conformity, non-believers generally value skepticism, individualism, and nonconformity. I inhabit both ends of that spectrum, sometimes finding meaning and comfort in religious traditions and sometimes feeling deeply skeptical of them. On self-reported personality measures, I receive high scores for extraversion and agreeability, qualities that correlate with religiousness, but like most atheists, I receive high scores for openness to experience. I consider myself both empathetic (an attribute shown to predict belief in God and quest orientation) and a rational thinker (a common characteristic in agnostics and atheists).

Interestingly, neuroimaging studies have provided evidence that empathy and analytic thinking involve two different brain networks—one activated by social and emotional tasks and the other activated by cognitively demanding tasks involving calculations, physical problem solving, or logical reasoning. These networks operate in opposition to each other; when one activates, the other deactivates. The scientists who conducted this study concluded that differences in "moral concern" (a construct that includes empathy and interpersonal connection) help explain why some people believe in God and why others don't. As a person who has worked hard to cultivate both compassion and reason, I'm curious how this tension has contributed to my way of being. Perhaps pursuing excellence in both domains means that I will never find a straight path to belief or disbelief. Perhaps I am destined to orbit them both, to feel the tug and release of gravity as I fly in endless figure eights.

Does God exist? What is the nature of reality? Is there a universal moral law? I doubt I'll ever find the answers to the ontological questions that preoccupy me. But certainty isn't the point—I see that now. After all, quests aren't really about accomplishing what you set out to do (at least the good ones aren't). Slaying the dragon, finding the oracle, rescuing the damsel in distress—those are just outposts along the road to actualization. Ultimately, quests are about becoming.

According to mythologist Joseph Campbell, the final stage of a hero's journey is "freedom to live." Having mastered spiritual and material realms, the hero is free to be whatever the journey has made her, unimpeded by regret or fear. And that's what this quest has really been about. Using science to investigate my religious experience has helped me embrace what I have become. It has convinced me that uncertainty is a gift, not a defect. Also, allowing my scientific and religious identities to work symbiotically has given me a more integrated sense of self.

Last Sunday began the Christian season of Advent, the four weeks of anticipation and preparation leading up to Christmas. For the occasion, my pastor preached on agnosticism—at least, that's the word she used, though I think she meant the kind of engaged "not knowing" that characterizes quest orientation. In the sermon, my pastor explained that she'd recently had a conversation with one of my fellow churchgoers (another quester, I suspect). The woman shared a secret: that she doesn't believe everything Christians are supposed to believe, but she never mentions this to anyone. So my pastor responded with these words for our congregation:

What if this Advent we let ourselves be agnostic, not knowing, and experience the gap between our knowledge and… God? Perhaps that gap, that Advent womb of unknowing, is where God's presence is made known, like the quickening of a child in her mother's body. Perhaps God prefers a bit of uncluttered space, a mind not yet resolved… This Advent, if you find yourself not knowing whether and how to believe in God, remember that you're not alone. The saints who have gone before us didn't register as agnostics, but they described a lot of unknowing, wondering, questions, and spiritual struggles. Throughout the Bible, God often works through people who are uncertain, who have no idea who God really is. And throughout the Bible, those who are overly-confident in their knowledge of God… are the ones who are spiritually stuck… Not knowing is not a bad thing. So let's enter Advent quietly, without knowing when or how God's desire to be with us will be fulfilled…

I felt grateful for her words, which I received as confirmation of what this quest has taught me: that I am free to live, to be what I am, to make uncertainty my home. What will I do with this newfound freedom? Explore. Expand my orbit. Seek out my fellow travelers so that we can share the weight and wonder of everything we do not know.

IN THE WOODS

Twelve hours after our cat Lyrock disappears, we stand on the deck behind our summer rental. Nate leans into the railing—shoulders hunched, head hanging. I pace the smooth wooden planks. Beside us, the bodies of moths beat against our kitchen windows. A humid wind hisses in the dense, dark canopy overhead. In the valley below, a tractor-trailer screams down Highway 36.

I wonder if Lyrock is injured or trapped. I imagine him pinned beneath a fallen tree or licking a bloody haunch in a neighbor's barn. I envision thick clumps of sand-colored fur strewn about the fallow field beyond our driveway.

When I wrap my arms around Nate, he shrugs me off.

"Do you blame me?" I ask.

He looks at me and says, "I'm trying not to."

Lyrock is out there, somewhere, in the patchwork farms, forests, and long-abandoned strip mines that surround us. This is the territory of Nate's boyhood. A place for throwing hatchets, making fires, and playing war games with the other children of pacifists. A place with sufficient thorns, ravines, and acidic ponds to make for thrilling nighttime missions.

We have chosen to spend our summers in this small community of Mennonite homesteaders because, for Nate, it is still home. His brother's farm is a mile hike through the woods, and his sister's family lives just up the hill—close enough that our five-year-old niece and two-year-old nephew sometimes show up, unaccompanied, to raid our candy drawer or invite me for a swim in the pond. A half-mile up the lane, Nate's parents inhabit the house he grew up in—a house his father built board by board, now flanked by mature fruit trees and lily ponds. Most evenings, we eat dinner with some or all of his family. Being here, I've learned to cook for and clean up after a hungry crowd of ten.

During these Ohio months, Nate works long days in his father's blacksmith shop, crafting kitchen and hunting knives. I spend my time reading, writing, and roaming the trails that crisscross the wooded acres between homes. Learning the intricacies of this place—the names of the frogs that chirp at dusk, the secret patches where chanterelles spring from the forest floor, the faint paths made by deer—feels like a form of intimacy, like tracing the palm of my sometimes inscrutable husband.

The morning after Lyrock disappears, Nate climbs out of bed soon after sunrise and pulls on his tattered work jeans. I dress, apply mosquito repellent, and follow him outside. We enter the strip of woods between our house and the cliff overlooking the highway. Beyond the weeds and brambles that border our yard, this stretch of forest feels surprisingly sparse, its floor carpeted with decaying leaves and intermittent ferns. Searching among columns of mature hardwoods, we duck beneath the webs of orb weavers, taking turns calling for Lyrock. At the foot of one tree, I stop to inspect the eerie white pipes of a corpse plant.

I should have listened to Nate last month, when I decided to start letting Lyrock outside. Our cat spent his first three years indoors, content enough to avoid the sirens, barking dogs, and raucous mobs of students in the Virginia college town where we live from August to May. But when we relocated to Ohio this summer, he began clawing the door and spraying the couch and carpet every time we went outside. I thought a limited diet of sunshine and fresh air would mellow him. Nate thought this place held too many dangers. Despite his hesitations, I let Lyrock out—at first under my supervision and then on his own, never for more than a few hours at a time. Just yesterday morning, I saw him reclining in the grass, gazing into the field beyond our gravel lane, breeze ruffling his mane.

While I zigzag through the woods, Nate walks fast along the ridgeline. He gets farther and farther ahead, and his calls grow faint. The distance between us worries me. If our fears come to pass—if Lyrock is dead or gone for good—what will that loss do to us? Losing a pet is a minor tragedy, but this already feels like a tear in the fabric of our marriage.

I've spent enough time in the land of grief to know that no one grieves the same way, and that a loved one's response to loss can be its own source of sorrow. Nate will undoubtedly withdraw from me. I've experienced it before, his animal response to pain, his desire to nurse his wounds in solitude and darkness. I am not like him. When I grieve, I crave human touch and words of reassurance. Learning to love each other has meant teaching ourselves to behave counter-intuitively, to offer our partners the inverse of our desires. But until now, our losses have been individual affairs. This shared grief is something new.

Three years ago, Nate followed me to Virginia, where I'd land-ed a professor gig. He took an adjunct teaching position that was bearable but uninspiring. Those first few months were especially hard, and I fretted over the disparity between the life Nate want-ed and the one he'd settled for because of me. Then we found a fluffy, blond kitten with enormous paws and golden eyes tumbling around a rescue display at Petco. And suddenly, there was a new source of joy in our house. I didn't worry about leaving Nate alone because Lyrock was there. Nate taught him to fetch a toy lobster and to jump five feet in the air and tag his hand for a treat. I'd come home to stories of wild chases and silly songs Nate com-posed about our cat. During arguments, Nate would diffuse ten-sion by saying, "At least we both love Lyrock. That's something."

When sheets of rain force us inside, I sob at the kitchen table. Nate walks upstairs. At least we are united in our concern, I tell myself. Our family and neighbors think we are out of our minds. They've all given us the same spiel: "Cats disappear, and then they come back days, sometimes weeks, later." We understand the sub-text: *Cats are just animals. It's not like you've lost a child.* Though they are right, Nate and I both feel stricken. We know that Lyrock isn't like the semi-feral cats around here. He never strays far from the house—and before now, he's never spent a night outdoors. The few times it stormed when he was outside, he arrived at the back door almost immediately—damp, panting, and yowling to be let indoors.

Nate and I feel the same sense of foreboding. Or maybe we don't. Because tangled up in my worry for our cat is a deeper fear: that by losing Lyrock here, I've not only stolen from Nate the thing that makes Virginia endurable but also corrupted this place, the home he loves and longs for.

We entertain out-of-town friends that morning and afternoon—forcing smiles, forcing food down our throats, trying to be gracious hosts despite our gnawing worry. As soon as they leave, we collapse on our bed.

"That was really hard for me," Nate says, his eyes filling.

"I know—it was for me too," I reply.

I recognize a defensive edge in my voice. All day, I've been apologizing to Nate. More than once, I've wailed into the ozone-laden air, "I'm sorry, Lyrock. I'm sorry." Shouldn't my repentance bring some measure of absolution? I feel desperate for mercy and comfort, and suspecting that Nate doubts my grief is more than I can bear.

Something stirs inside of me—that old anger I used as both sword and shield in my first marriage. It would be so easy, at this moment, to turn on each other, to strike at each other's exposed underbellies. But I know how that story ends.

I take a deep breath and say to Nate, "Let's be kind to each other, okay?"

"Okay," he says, rolling toward me.

Then we hold each other and cry. We also puzzle over Lyrock's disappearance. He couldn't have been hit by a car or stolen—this is the middle of nowhere. Coyotes and bobcats don't hunt during the day. Could a hawk have gotten him? Could he have run away? Nothing makes sense.

Over the next couple of days, we redouble our efforts to find Lyrock or any sign of what happened to him. Between thunderstorms that dump inches of rain, turning gravel roads into rivers, we make wider and wider circles around the property. We walk along the highway and scour our neighbors' barns and outbuildings, sweat-drenched in the sultry summer heat.

We've never spent so much time on this land together. Usually, I travel alone, though Nate's father has been my tour guide on occasion—showing me a rare wild ginseng and the towering trunks of the largest poplars on the property. He was the one who taught me about the licorice-flavored clusters of sweet cicely that bloom along the trails in early summer. But now, it's Nate who is pointing out the bullet-riddled mound of dirt at the end of his neighbor's gun range and the remains of an old kiln built into the hillside. Even in the fog of worry, it is easy to see why he is pulled to this earth, these trees, these hills that roll into the winding Tuscarawas River. I feel their pull too.

Still, I'm not ready to give myself to this place, to make it my home in the yellow days of autumn and the long gray of winter and muddy churning of spring. The people who live here have chosen community over careers, reliance on the earth and each other over independence. Giving myself to this place would mean becoming dependent on Nate, his family, and their neighbors. There is goodness in that possibility, I know—the promise of roots and of deep connections to people and place. But I've worked hard to build an identity and prospects that my husband can't yank out from under me. That's what happened when my first husband left me, and I've vowed not to make that mistake again. Though I long for the kind of belonging this place offers, if we made this place our life and the tether that binds me to Nate broke, I could lose everything—my marriage, our community, the ground beneath my feet. Right now, losing a cat feels hard enough.

While we search, we talk about Lyrock. Could he have eaten something poisonous? Could he have crawled into a hole or burrow and gotten stuck? If he is alive, we wonder if he's managed to find anything to eat. Occasionally, he bats clumsy moths to the floor, but he's failed to kill any of the mice that regularly climb from the crawlspace of our rental into the downstairs bathroom through a hole beneath the sink. At least he will have water to drink—that's the one good thing about all the rain.

Our hope that we will find him alive or that he will return— sodden and covered in leaves, but whole—gradually gives way to the fear that we will find what is left of him—a carcass with its belly torn open, a flattened mass on the highway, or a few telltale tufts of fur. Or what if we never find him? Would not knowing what happened be worse than finding him dead?

The third morning after Lyrock's disappearance, we methodically crisscross the field near our house, searching for remains. Wading through tall grass and wildflowers, I spy wolf spiders, twin jewel beetles, a praying mantis, a differential grasshopper, and a rabbit—but no Lyrock. Seeking the scent of death, I find instead the heady fragrance of wild roses and a rich dankness at the edge of the forest. When we finish, I head into town to buy spray bottles and tuna fish to make "chum trails" that might lead Lyrock home, if he is lost—free advice we've received from a kind-hearted "pet detective" we found online. Nate trudges west, wearing two pairs of pants to protect himself from thorns and carrying a freshly sharpened machete to hack through the underbrush.

When I return from the store, the house is empty. I stand in the kitchen, staring. Then, the screen door creaks, and I turn to see Nate's face, flushed and sweat-streaked.

"I found his body," he says.

I gasp. "No! No! No!"

"And it's alive!" Nate proclaims, stepping inside. In his arms rests Lyrock, purring. My beloved cat is back, and so is Nate's dark sense of humor.

Nate tells me he found him cowering beneath a briar thicket on a neighbor's land—beyond fields and a stream, about a half-mile from our house. He responded to one of Nate's calls with a meow. When Nate came closer, Lyrock emerged from his hideout and leapt into his arms.

"Maybe a dog chased him over there, and he couldn't find his way back," Nate suggests.

"I can't believe you found him," I say. "I really thought he was dead."

"I know," Nate replies. "I just couldn't give up."

We ponder the odds. Within a half-mile radius of our house, there are hundreds of acres of dense vegetation. It feels miraculous that Nate walked within fifty feet of Lyrock.

That night, we pile into bed together. Lyrock, who is not typically a cuddler, lies between us, resting his chin on my shoulder. I bask in the joy and relief of our reunion. And there is this too: the reassurance that Nate and I were kind, as we promised to be. During our three-day ordeal, we listened and responded to each other's suggestions. We did not blame or bicker or lash out. I managed not to spin my anxiety into anger. Nate remained affectionate, rather than retreating to his inner fortress. That we loved each other well gives me hope, though I recognize the need for caution. Our grief had barely hatched when it met its end. Who can say what kind of beast it might have grown into?

Still, I feel less afraid than I did before Lyrock disappeared—less afraid that I'll destroy what I love, less afraid that my husband will abandon me, less afraid to let this place into my bones.

Outside, bats are diving for mosquitoes in the weak starlight. The crescent moon has already set, and the fireflies have concluded their nightly show. I listen to moths drumming the illumined panels of our bedroom windows, their wings beating back the dark.

TRAIL TIME

Standing here in the deep, brooding silence all the wilderness seems motionless, as if the work of creation were done. But in the midst of this outer steadfastness we know there is incessant motion and change.

—JOHN MUIR, "Mount Ritter"

We arrive at Roads End Ranger Station at 11 a.m. on a Sunday morning. Nate and I have flown from Ohio to California and driven over the golden hills surrounding the San Francisco Bay, through Central Valley orchards, and beneath giant sequoias on the western slopes of the Sierra Nevada. We spent the last hour negotiating hairpin curves as we dropped into a canyon cleaved by the south fork of the Kings River.

The ranger behind the counter has strawberry blonde hair and freckles, and she strikes me as very young. While my husband and I wait for a backpacking permit, I watch her dispense with a series of visitors. She answers their questions succinctly, her gaze intense, her voice stern.

Do I need a permit to day hike? No—only for multiday trips in the backcountry.

Should we report bear sightings? Not unless the bear was aggressive.

Are there free trail maps? No—they're sold at the bookstore near the campground.

Following her recitation of the rules for human waste disposal and campsite selection, she gives a couple of trekkers a pop quiz on the details.

"Remember," she reminds them before they go, "protect the bears from your food."

Something about her reminds me of myself at age twenty-two. Maybe it's her seriousness, which I read as an attempt to convince everyone—maybe even herself—that she knows what she's doing.

"Is this your first season?" I ask her after the crowds clear.

"Yes." She tells me she'll be here in Kings Canyon until September and then transfer to another park to the north.

I ask what drew her to the job, and I learn that she recently graduated from an Ivy League university, where she wrote her thesis on the bureaucratic functioning of the National Park Service (or something along those lines). Working as a ranger is a way to experience what she's been studying, she explains. I tell her about the summer I spent as a backpacking guide in Yosemite a few years back, and we swap strategies for managing the inevitable fear that accompanies camping alone in the backcountry: Hike so hard you fall asleep before dark. Limit how much you drink in the evenings so that you don't have pee in the middle of the night. Make camp in the same places—there's comfort in familiarity. She suggests that I read Eric Blehm's *The Last Season*, and I tell her about Roderick Nash's *Wilderness and the American Mind*. Each of us writes down the other's recommendation in a little notebook.

We talk for half an hour, maybe more, until it's time for her lunch break.

"A kindred spirit," I whisper to my husband as she shutters the station.

With envy, I watch her walk into the pines.

Eleven years ago, when I was her age, I married my college sweetheart—followed him to the foothills of North Carolina so that he could study theology. Suddenly responsible for providing for two adults, I took the first job I interviewed for: English teacher at a small parochial school. This was a mistake, I quickly realized. Not only did I have no teaching experience, none of my seven classes had a syllabus or curriculum, and several had no textbooks. The administration seemed more concerned with how I would integrate Bible verses into each lesson than with whether or not their students could write a coherent paragraph. Still, I was determined to do right by my students and finish the school year. Every day, I came home exhausted and demoralized, with stacks of papers to grade. My husband, on the other hand, came home energized by new ideas. He tossed around big words like ontology and eschatology and seemed to have an abundance of spare time, which he used to go for walks, smoke a tobacco pipe on our back porch, and join his friends for drinks at local bars.

Resentment is a potent poison. How might my life have been different if I'd taken a job as a park ranger at age twenty-two instead of becoming a wife and teacher? Maybe I would have discovered the joys of self-reliance, hard physical labor, and mindfulness years sooner. Maybe my first love and I would have recognized the many ways we were mismatched and spared ourselves a failed marriage. He could have gone off to fight wildfires in Oregon, like he'd talked about doing early in our relationship (a dream I stomped out like an errant ember). Perhaps I'd have had a few love affairs that would've taught me more about what I needed in a partner and could give to a relationship. Undoubtedly, I'd have more adventure stories to tell.

In the morning, Nate and I set off with everything we need for five days in the wilderness strapped to our backs. We cross a footbridge over a turquoise stretch of the Kings River and navigate a series of switchbacks through oak scrub. Twice, we narrowly avoid rattlesnakes camouflaged by the sun-dappled dust of the trail.

In our first two hours, we cover four miles and gain 1,500 feet of elevation, but our pace slows over the course of the day. Seven hours into our trek, I begin to worry. We haven't reached the junction to East Lake, which means that we're still more than two miles from Vidette Meadow, where we hope to camp. I peer through the trees to the cliffs on either side of Bubbs Creek, attempting to judge the distance between them. According to my map, the valley gets flatter and wider just before the junction. The walls appear to have opened a bit, but I can't be sure. It's also possible that the map is wrong—topography isn't an exact science, and signposts have already revealed a few discrepancies—so there's no telling how much farther it is to the junction or to our camp.

I hope we're close, though, because my swollen feet have started to blister, and my shoulders ache beneath my heavy pack. Nate is out of water, and soon, I will be too. We're both drenched in sweat and coated in a fine layer of brown dust. It wouldn't be a bad idea to stop for a snack and to collect some water, but I'm determined to make it to the junction first. As we trudge onward, I can feel my chest tightening, my breathing growing more rapid.

Nate notices and asks if I want to stop.

"Shut up," I say. "I just want to get to the junction."

I take a few deep, deliberately slow breaths to calm myself down. I see what's happening, and I don't like it. My desperate need to get to some arbitrary point on the map is, in fact, pointless.

It belies many of the reasons I go backpacking: to slow down, to escape my schedule and obligations, to enjoy nature and my husband's company, to exist in the present. There is no rush. My body is strong and capable of what I'm asking it to do. We're equipped to hike in the dark, if we must. Why wish away time I will never get back?

And why risk spoiling Nate's experience of this place—or this activity? He wasn't much of a trekker before we started dating, and I told him early on that loving me would require spending time in the woods. He's seemed to enjoy the hikes and backpacking trips we've taken together over the last five years, but he's also quiet and uncomplaining. I sometimes wonder if he'd rather be doing something else. I want him to love backpacking—or at least to like it enough to continue taking treks with me—which means that I need to be an amiable companion.

I apologize for my outburst, and few minutes later, we reach the junction, where we pause to eat granola bars and reapply mosquito repellent. Sufficiently refreshed, we continue our ascent. Before long, the trees open up, and we glimpse the snowcapped peaks that inspired the name of this mountain range. The trail grows steep, but our reward is an open view of the creek, parting around boulders, swirling through eddies, tumbling down cascades. The deep notes of river on rock fill the air; the vibrations dance on my skin. Behind us, the canyon drops away, carpeted in green. We stop, again, to replenish our water supply and stand awestruck near the lip of a waterfall, watching the evening light pool and spill over the rim.

Then we walk, winding between boulders, ankles brushing bright red tufts of alpine paintbrush. A mother grouse and her chicks eye us from the side of the trail. At this hour, blue shadows elongate across the gorge. The mountains exhale, banishing the afternoon heat. Where it can still reach, the low-slung sun paints the granite gold. I am rapt beneath my pack. If I could, I would stop time. I'd dwell in this perfect millisecond a while longer.

The next morning, my clothes are still wet with sweat, so I arrange them on a rock to dry in the sun. Our campsite—a peninsula of high, sandy ground in lush meadow—affords a lovely view of the jagged Vidette Peaks to the south and Kearsarge Pinnacles to the west; but the mosquitoes are relentless. Nate and I swat at them as we munch Cliff Bars and sip steaming cups of instant coffee. Then we tear down our tent and stuff our gear into our packs.

Almost immediately after setting off, we intersect the John Muir Trail, which we take northbound toward Rae Lakes. Nate reminds me to pace myself. We've gained nearly a mile of elevation since beginning our trek yesterday, and we've got close to 2,500 vertical feet to go before we reach Glen Pass, which will be the literal high point of our trip at 11,978 feet above sea level. Nate knows my tendency to push hard early and drag later on, and he's better at monitoring exertion and conserving energy, which I appreciate. I step aside and let him set our speed.

Over the next several hours, we crisscross the steep flank of Mount Bago, traverse a sandy bowl east of Charlotte Lake, and pick our way up a series of rocky switchbacks. We pause to catch our breath and admire an alpine lake guarded by a sheer cliff—the water is an intense shade of blue neither of us has ever seen. A little while later, we hear a loud crack, and we turn to see rocks tumbling down the cliff and landing on a snowbank hundreds of feet below. At last, we reach the serrated saddle of Glen Pass, where we stare into a horizon fractured by sharp peaks. Below us, lakes pool in basins carved by glaciers, sapphires glittering in granite settings.

I search my memory for the first time I heard about the man for whom this trail was named—"John of the Mountains," famed nineteenth century adventurer, defender of wilderness, and co-founder of the Sierra Club. Before I profiled John Muir for a nature writing class or thumbed through his collected writings in a Yosemite National Park bookstore, he came to me in song. I was eighteen years old—a college freshman on a weekend retreat in the Blue Ridge Mountains—and a musician named Ryan Long sang a ballad he'd composed about Muir. The song recounted the time Muir climbed a Douglas fir in the middle of a windstorm. Strumming his guitar with mounting urgency, Long sang: *He said I will not run away from the wind / Or hold up in your cabin where it cannot seep in / I want to hike the highest ridge and climb the tallest tree / And hold on for dear life to feel the wind in me.* At the time, I found Muir's reckless passion romantic (so did the songwriter, apparently). Here was someone who knew how to live to the fullest, how to seize the day, how to suck the marrow out of life.

Later, when I stumbled across a colorized photograph of young Muir—piercing blue eyes framed by a dark mop of hair and a thick, unruly beard—my admiration for the historical figure morphed into a full-fledged crush. I devoured his writings—stories of his childhood in Scotland, his puritanical upbringing in rural Wisconsin, and the accident that ultimately set him a-wandering at the age of twenty-nine. In the spring of 1867, at the factory where he worked, a metal file punctured one of those beautiful blue eyes, and the aqueous humors dripped from his cornea into his open hand. Within hours, his uninjured eye also went dark.

Muir was uncertain whether he would recover his vision, but he did—and sight restored, he could no longer resist the call of "wild nature."

Muir's tales of his time in the Sierra beguiled me most: While working at a sawmill and hotel in Yosemite Valley, he built himself a cabin with a stream running through it (what whimsy!). He explored the high country for weeks at a time—often with no blanket and only a bit of bread to eat—and climbed several of the tallest peaks in the West (what pluck!). When Ralph Waldo Emerson visited Yosemite in 1871, Muir played tour guide and was sorely disappointed when the celebrity's guardian insisted he stay in a hotel, rather than camping with Muir in a grove of giant sequoias (poor Johnny!). Muir—who wrote of trees, flowers, and waterfalls with a wonderment akin to worship—inspired my first pilgrimage to Yosemite the summer I turned twenty-one. There, I walked several miles on the northernmost section of the John Muir Trail and thought longingly of Muir the naturalist, Muir the mountaineer, Muir the poet.

On this trip, more than a decade later, my imagination summons a different Muir. The ghost over my shoulder wears the gray-streaked beard of Muir the husband, Muir the activist, Muir the elder. Although famous for his wilderness adventures, Muir lived in the Sierra for fewer than six years before he started wintering in Oakland. By his late thirties, the Bay Area had become his year-round residence, and from then on, he seldom visited the Sierra for more than a month at a time. As Donald Worster, one of Muir's biographers, concedes, "He stretched those Sierra years into a myth of eternal youth, so that in all of his subsequent writings it would seem that he had never left the mountains."

How does someone so deeply in love with a place choose to leave it? Maybe the loneliness got to him. By all accounts, Muir was a riveting storyteller, a thought-provoking conversationalist, and an ardent debater. Perhaps he loved people as much, or more, than mountains.

That night, we camp on a mile-long strip of land that divides the upper and middle Rae Lakes. The air is relatively warm, and the sky is clear, so we leave the rain fly off the tent. I inhale the chalky fragrance of granite dust, the clean tang of pine needles, and something else—the faint scent of smoke from last night's campfire, lingering in Nate's hair. Swaddled in my sleeping bag, I stare through mesh. Fin Dome towers over the westernmost lake, black against the blue remnants of twilight. Its humped profile reminds me of a headstone.

Who can know a man's heart (especially one that stopped beating more than a century ago)? I make no such claim. But I find myself wondering about the yearnings that warred beneath John Muir's breastbone. How did he reconcile his hunger for adventure with his desire for a family—a desire consummated in his marriage to Louisa Strentzel, heiress to an agricultural estate in the Alhambra Valley? He once wrote that the Sierra was his "true home." Does that mean he never felt at home on the ranch and fruit farm where his daughters learned to walk and speak and run? Did he take pleasure in the work of writing and advocacy that increasingly occupied his hours? These endeavors ensured the preservation of the wilds he loved, but they also tethered him to civilization.

I'd like to know this, too: how does aging affect a man like Muir? Although he made excursions into the wilderness for most of his life, the records show a scaling back in scope, a tapering of activity leading up to his death from pneumonia at the age of seventy-six. What was it like to witness the bones and joints and muscles that carried him to the summit of Mount Whitney becoming fragile and weak? In his dreams of the Sierra, did he walk with a cane or inhabit a young man's frame?

The next day, Nate and I take a side trip to Sixty Lakes Basin, a destination recommended by the young ranger at Road's End. We leave our gear in camp and climb up the ridge west of Rae Lakes. Purple flowers—shooting stars—congregate near streams, and yellow-bellied marmots scurry behind rocks. In the basin, we explore a series of graduated bowls filled by lakes. The first reflects patches of snow on the steep cirque surrounding it. The next lake is larger, and its golden orange shallows transition to turquoise and, eventually, midnight blue at the interior. We follow that lake's outlet and eventually end up in a boggy vale studded with boulders and small, jewel-colored tarns.

At midday, we turn back. Our descent provides us a bird's eye view of the long valley that stretches north from Rae Lakes. We search for and find the dome of our tent on the isthmus—an orange speck near a cluster of boulders. Below us, the thin thread of the John Muir Trail divides meadows, crosses slopes, and disappears into stands of evergreens.

This isn't my first time traversing the thirteen miles between Vidette Meadow (where we camped the first night) and the cable bridge over Woods Creek (which we will cross tomorrow).

Eight years ago, my first husband and I passed through this valley on a southbound thru-hike of the John Muir Trail. I keep having moments where time collapses, like an accordion. I inhabit two places at once—or rather, two times in one place. One moment, Nate leans over a rock to fill a bottle with water. A second later, my first husband scoops a trout out of the lake and unhooks his fly from its jaw. I can almost touch the fluttering gills, stroke the speckled scales of its flexed body. I reach out, and my fingers meet the chilled plastic of the water bottle.

Then, like an accordion, time expands. The streaked visage of The Painted Lady, the sound of the wind rushing through rocks, the earthy scent of the dust on my skin and pack and clothes—all of these are the same as they were eight years ago. But I am not. At thirty-three, I've got gray hair, wrinkles, and age spots. I've survived divorce, graduate school, job loss, and the death of a parent. I am not the twenty-five-year-old who constantly complained about her blisters and the weight of her pack and her exhaustion. I'm not the needy wife who expected her husband to solve the problem of her discomfort—or the girl who would deliberately drag her feet and then, after banging her toes on rocks, whip herself into frenzies of frustration.

"Did I leave him with any good memories?" I wonder aloud.

Nate doesn't attempt to speak for the man I used to call husband. We walk in silence, and I take comfort in that silence. I do not want to be consoled or questioned or even complimented. It is enough to see our shadows side by side, moving in synchrony.

Why return to this place, crowded as it is with apparitions from my past? Partly because I love the Sierra. Even in the midst of self-imposed misery, its beauty beguiled me. And partly, too, because I want to share it with the man I love. Maybe it's also about covering familiar ground with kindness and being the companion that I wish I had been. One place, two times—two times, one place.

In the afternoon, Nate and I hike several more miles with our packs and make our third camp on a rise above Dollar Lake. Eight years ago, I stopped at this spot for a snack and, later in the day, watched my first husband jump off a rock into one of Rae Lakes. My aversion to cold water kept me from joining him. In fact, I declined to swim in any of the alpine lakes I passed on our thru-hike—and there were hundreds of them, pristine pools of different sizes and shapes and shades.

When Nate suggests we go for a dip, I agree to join him. I wade into the clear, cold water, chasing the retreating sunrays. Trout glide past me, rising to the smooth surface to snag mosquitoes. I get about thigh deep before the rocky floor drops away. My entire body bristles with goosebumps. I stop and turn to the shore, where Nate is stripping off his clothes.

"It's cold," he says, when he walks into water.

Then, without warning, he dives into the depths. Earlier today, he told me that the bottomless blue of these mountain lakes fills him with unease. I couldn't quite figure out what he meant— only that it was something in between the fear I felt swimming in Florida's alligator-infested lakes throughout my childhood and the existential dread I sometimes experience when I look into the night sky and ponder the dimensions of the universe.

But here he is now, propelling himself toward that dark unknown. I smile at his courage and am glad when he rises, whooping and laughing.

"Come on!" he calls.

I take a breath, count to three, and hurl myself toward the center, toward Nate, toward the gilded Sierra reflected in that unfathomable deep.

On the fourth morning of our trip—our last full day on the trail—we descend alongside the South Fork of Woods Creek. I watch the creek expand and pick up speed, and I wonder where the water in this current originated. Some surely melted off of Glen Pass and flowed through Rae and Dollar Lakes. Some spilled out of Sixty Lakes Basin. Maybe it came down as rain and wetted crags unseen by human eyes. Maybe it dusted the fur of a mountain lion as snow. There may be a thousand provenances represented here, or a million—a different story for each molecule, drawn by gravity and topography to its brethren. This water—the aggregate of innumerable drops—has sustained trout and frogs and has parted around the feet of deer, bears, and hikers. Its surface has held ridges illumined by alpenglow and thunderheads pregnant with rain and electricity. On windless nights, it has mirrored the shimmering arc of the Milky Way, fusing it into a ring.

Nate and I move quickly and breathe easy on this downhill stretch. On either side of us, gnarled cedars cling to rocky moraines that border the valley. Stone spires—12,000 and 13,000 feet tall—loom to the north. Beneath them, waterfalls tumble down mountainsides. The wind carries their rumbling across the great, open expanse before us. After four miles, we dip beneath conifer canopy. The trail crosses Woods Creek on a narrow cable bridge—a complex assembly of wood and wire. "One person at a time," a sign warns. The bridge shudders and sways under me, gaps between its slats revealing white water below.

The time has come to leave the John Muir Trail. It proceeds north, all the way to Yosemite, but we will follow Woods Creek west. I feel a prick of sorrow: *When will I return? What if I never return?* I have such thoughts every time I leave the Sierra. In a world full of beautiful places, do you revisit the ones that mark you or seek out new ones to explore? And life happens—we may not always have the time or money or health required to spend a week or more in the woods. Muir's first summer in the Sierra became the stuff of legend—it filled a book. But what about his final trip to the Sierra? One of those jaunts was his last. One will be ours too. I just hope it's not this trip.

Beneath a blazing sun, we weave our way through trunks charred by fire. There are cacti here, and scarlet penstemon, and the broad white blossoms of cow parsnip. At the head of Paradise Valley, foot-long sugar pine cones clutter the ground.

I am still thinking about the red-headed ranger—maybe because Nate has accumulated a list of questions to ask her when we get back: What is the maximum elevation for bears? Are the pods of those bean-looking plants edible? Do rattlesnakes make their own holes or occupy other animals' burrows? What do rangers eat when they're in the backcountry?

Nate inquires what I'll ask the ranger if we see her again.

"For her email address," I joke. "I wish we were friends."

I'm still experiencing twinges of envy—though I've realized what I covet is not so much the path she has chosen but her youth. Her adulthood stretches out before her—a large, blank map with infinite possibilities for adventure and exploration. I am hardly a decade older than she is, but each of those years has cropped the margins of my map. Choosing one trail has usually required forsaking others—abandoning, even, whole territories.

Up ahead, just out of sight, a junction waits for me—and Nate too. We can stay on this trail—one that affords us the time to take week-long treks in the backcountry and the option to fill our hours with thinking and writing. Or we can veer left and start a family, exchanging the unknowns that lie ahead for a different set of unknowns. Having a child—or children—might mean that I won't return to the John Muir trail for years, or maybe never. But not having a child would mean giving up the opportunity to experience community, family, and my body in new ways. We don't have to decide right now, but the choice won't always be there. Or maybe it has already passed us by, and we don't even know it. What I want is to take both paths at once, to retain my freedom and mobility and know deep connection to a creature who inhabited my womb and nursed at my breast.

It occurs to me why Muir the elder is the Muir I've conjured on this trip. Muir of the hoary beard is the foil to my young ranger. His map is complete. And I stand somewhere in between, wondering what it means to live a good life. I cannot say how Muir felt, in the end, about the proportions of time he spent roaming the Sierra, communing with other people, and writing at his desk. But I am grateful for the hours and days he allotted to each. Were it not for his love of these mountains and his dedication to defending them, this place may have been lost. Without his words—tenderly crafted for his fellow humans—I may not have found my way here.

Nate and I set up our final camp in a sandy bowl on the northern bank of Woods Creek. Our long descent has left our bodies weary—today we lost 4,000 feet of elevation over fourteen miles in 90-degree heat. In the morning, we will rise early and walk the six remaining miles to our car. Part of me is looking forward to a hot shower and a hamburger. Another part of me wants to remain in the Sierra with Nate forever.

We decide to eat our last freeze-dried dinner on a boulder in the middle of the creek.

"Are you glad we're here?" I ask.

Nate looks up from his foil pouch and nods. "It's been a good trip."

Beside us, shallow water moves gently over polished stones. We sit in shadow, dwarfed by enormous fir trees that line the banks like columns. Beyond the forest, 3,000-foot canyon walls enclose Paradise Valley. We're facing downstream, toward the valley's narrow outlet, above which Buck Peak has caught the light of the setting sun.

"I wonder how long this spot has looked like this," I say.

"Probably a long time," Nate replies.

It is easy to imagine John Muir—or the indigenous people who lived here until the mid-nineteenth century—inhabiting this scene: stooping for a drink, collecting firewood. But the Sierra is changing, a truth evinced by every peak and valley, rock and river in this range. Human civilizations rise and fall in the span of centuries, but a millennium is a mountain's yawn. Muir knew this. He saw in these mountains "the eternal flux of Nature manifested."

The granite serving as our perch and table tonight is somewhere between eighty million and 200 million years old. Dinosaurs still roamed the earth when it burst as hot magma into subterranean chambers, where it cooled and was eventually exposed by erosion. The lofty peaks came later—this range is young, as far as mountains go. About ten million years ago, the fault block that runs the length of California began rising, while the plate to the east began sinking. As a result, the western side of the Sierra rises gently from the Central Valley, while the eastern escarpment towers precipitously over the Owens Valley. The Sierra is still rising one or two millimeters a year—which in mountain time is a pretty brisk pace (and in my lifetime will amount to roughly four inches). We're camping in a valley carved by a glacier that formed during the last ice age. Twenty thousand years ago, only the pinnacles of these mountains would have stood above the ice—monuments in a vast, frozen sea.

Contemplating the geologic history of this place is like staring into the dark center of a lake. It's impossible to fully grasp time on such a scale, to understand the unfolding of ages. We are that orange speck of a tent on the isthmus. No, we are drops of water in the lake—two provenances united, infinitesimally small but also part of this place where destruction and creation, violence and stillness, rising and falling are one and the same. Together, we wade into this mystery. We plunge into the unfathomable deep.

ISLAND, WILDING

From the ferry's observation deck, we watch the sleepy port of St. Marys recede. Beyond the brackish water churning in our wake, the gray December sky hangs low over a winter-gold marsh. I inhale the scents of mud, salt, and sea, grateful for the wind on my cheeks and for a moment's reprieve from the nausea that has accompanied my first trimester of pregnancy.

It's been more than a decade since my last visit to Cumberland Island, a 17.5-mile long barrier island just north of the Florida-Georgia border. Accessible only by water or air, it offers adventurers 9,800 acres of designated wilderness and more than fifty miles of trails. In both high school and college, I led friends on backpacking trips there. We chased armadillos through its maritime forests, waded through tidal creeks, and trekked barefooted over miles of deserted beaches. This time, I've brought my husband and my brother with me—and the tiny being, no bigger than a lime, that's floating in my womb. But I'm not sure what, exactly, I'm taking them to.

Three months ago, Hurricane Irma tore through this region, sinking boats, downing trees, and ripping docks from their moorings. The National Park Service evacuated Cumberland Island and closed it to visitors for weeks of cleanup and restoration, just as it did last year after Hurricane Matthew damaged its docks, trails, and beaches. I know that natural disasters like these are likely to multiply and intensify as a result of our changing climate. Rising, warming seas are already lapping up the edges of islands everywhere, which makes me wonder: how do I raise a child in this world, knowing such destruction will be his inheritance?

Relief fills me when we disembark at Sea Camp dock. The majestic live oaks of my memory remain, unscathed. Thick branches bow toward the sandy soil, forming living archways, benches, and slides. Other limbs, draped in Spanish moss, spiral upward and divide into an intricate lacework overhead. Beneath the canopy, the fanned fronds of saw palmetto form a nearly impenetrable understory. We shoulder our packs and set off on a silvery trail cut through the bright green blades. After half a mile, we reach our campsite—a clearing with a fire ring, picnic table, and a cage on a post, designed to keep our food from the nimble paws of raccoons. To the east, massive sand dunes border the canopy. We can't see the Atlantic Ocean over the powdery, white mounds, but we can hear its waves crashing on the beach.

Interspersed throughout the campground are mature citrus trees, heavy with oranges, grapefruits, tangerines, and kumquats. My husband and brother sneak into neighboring campsites and scale twisted trunks, plucking bright orbs and shaking others to the ground. They return with a bounty, their fingers scented with zest, and we feast on tart wedges. This abundance surprises me. How is it that the hurricane didn't rip the hard, green fruits from their boughs?

I wonder, too, who planted these trees. This island has a long history of human habitation. Indigenous peoples hunted, fished, and occupied villages here for thousands of years. Spanish and British colonizers built forts on the island, and later, plantation owners used slaves to raise livestock, harvest timber, and grow cash crops like cotton and indigo here. Pittsburgh millionaire Thomas Carnegie (brother of Andrew Carnegie) acquired an estate here in the 1880s, and in the following decades, his family purchased 90 percent of the island and built several mansions as winter retreats. I suppose it was one of the Carnegie employees who put these trees in the ground and tended them in their early, vulnerable years. Could he have imagined that the fruits of his labor would delight the tongues of hungry hikers more than a century later? I envy the legacy he unwittingly nurtured.

After making camp, we walk south on the beach, stopping to examine the vacant carapaces of horseshoe crabs and patterns carved in the sand by the outbound tide. A flock of seagulls scours a shallow pool near the shore, then ascends in a chaotic whorl. With a mile of boot-prints behind us, we turn inland and take a boardwalk through a swamp interspersed with cabbage palms. Here, we see the first of many feral horses—a white mare who, despite her dingy coat, looks like she wandered out of a fairy tale. She is a descendant of the mounts brought here by the British in the eighteenth century and, given her coloring, perhaps of one of the Arabians the Carnegies turned loose, hoping to improve the wild stock enough to domesticate and sell.

A little while later, we arrive at Dungeness, the estate of Thomas and Lucy Carnegie. We stand before the ruins of their mansion, completed in 1884. Crumbling brick and stone walls, towering chimneys, and hollow portals are all that's left of the opulent fifty-nine-room castle. Gone are the lavish fixtures and furniture. Gone are the elites who golfed, hunted, and dined here as guests of one of America's wealthiest families. Gone are the nearly

200 servants who once maintained the estate. All it took was a single spark, in 1959, to consume the years of planning and labor (and the sizable fortune) required to construct the 35,000-square-foot edifice. It gives me a strange pleasure to know that the island's horses, considered inferior by Thomas Carnegie, have outlasted his mansion by more than twenty generations.

I continue thinking about the Dungeness mansion—grass sprouting through its cracked foundation, vines snaking up its interior walls—as we hike back to camp through the forest. I think about it as we roast kebabs over our campfire. I think about it after I retire early to our tent, the fluids in my body churning like the ocean beyond the dunes. Every parent is an architect, bent on shaping the world around her children so that they—and their children—will thrive. Wasn't that what Lucy Carnegie was doing when she oversaw the construction of her castle, then funded three more Cumberland Island mansions for her married children? Whatever world she was trying to create for them isn't here anymore.

In the morning, we pedal rented bicycles up the road that bisects the island, whirring through a long, green tunnel on white sand. Miles north, we pass through fragrant pine groves and over a brackish creek. Eventually, we reach Plum Orchard—the classical revival style mansion built for George Carnegie and later occupied by his sister Nancy and her husband, the island's doctor. Inside, we pass through rooms clad in hand-painted wallpaper and ornate wood paneling. A tour guide points out the innovative plumbing in one of the mansion's twelve bathrooms and shows us the coal furnace used to heat the indoor swimming pool. Here, we get a glimpse into the Carnegies' extravagant lifestyle. But for me, the dark hallways and stuffy air evoke decay. I am eager to return to the live oaks and salt breeze outside.

Soon, we are speeding south alongside the surf. Long shadows spill from our bicycles and intertwine as we race past each other. Wheeling over the hard sand, sunlight glinting on the waves, I am overcome with joy. For the moment, I inhabit a world worth leaving to the being Nate and I have created. I throw my head back and shout, "I'm having a baby!"

We spend the final night of our trip stargazing on the beach. In the morning, after a simple breakfast of coffee and granola bars, we collapse our tents and return to the Sea Camp dock. Waiting to board the ferry, I watch a pair of parents chase their grubby one-year-old over gnarled oak roots. I smile at them and think, yes. The key to raising a child in a world permeated with destruction is to choose wilderness over walls. For in the face of fires and floods, fortresses crumble. But the beings that become part of the wild, rather than attempting to subdue or resist it, beget life. The citrus trees and horses here testify to that truth.

I will not be able to spare my child this planet's brokenness any more than I can save this island from the rising seas. Who knows what will surround this seed I am planting half a century from now. But I can teach him to love birds and beasts and trees. I can teach him to learn from them and live in peace with them. And I can take comfort in this: wherever there is wilderness, there is life.

AFTER BIRTH:

THE POSTPARTUM BEDROOM
IN SEVEN TAKES

---

1. Den. In the days following the birth, there is no escaping the animal smell of my bedroom. My clothes stink of leaked breastmilk and musky, hormone-laden sweat. Every now and then, I inhale the tang of my own blood. Another soiled diaper awaits removal. But I lean in and bask in this: the lemony fragrance of wild roses rising off your skin.

2. Temple. The afternoon light streams onto the bed, where you doze beside me. I stare at you—this being I have made—feeling completely unmade by your long eyelashes, your velvety earlobes, and your toenails, tiny as glass beads. In the soft spot atop your head, your pulse leaps, quick and miraculous.

3. Torture chamber. Bone weary, I search for an impossible solution. I cradle you, balance you face-down on my forearm, then prop you against my shoulder, stroking the downy fringe at the base of your skull. I try bouncing, stepping, dipping, and turning. I memorize the creaky floorboards. When, at last, you sleep in the bassinet beside my bed, I find it impossible to close my eyes. I count your breaths and, when they become slow and shallow, hover a hand over you, waiting for your belly to meet my palm.

4. **Tree house.** Our bedroom windows overlook the tree-tops on this Appalachian ridge. Today, as a thunderstorm approaches, I watch their chaotic dance. The oaks, maples, aspens, and locusts move asynchronously, as if possessed by different spirits. Oblivious to the din outside, you sleep on my chest. I consider retreating below, worried that the blighted ash beside the house might release its grip on the earth. I also consider waking you and lifting you to the glass so that you, too, might witness the whirling, thrashing, and trembling of the trees.

5. **School.** Lessons learned: How to fold a diaper so it doesn't rub the tender stump of your umbilicus. How to suckle you while I sleep, arms and knees encircling the half-moon of your body. How to trim your fingernails, soft and thin as rice paper. How to clean the creases in your neck. How to inhabit a body that has been suddenly and violently vacated.

6. **Refuge.** I remember the story of O-Lan in *The Good Earth*, who returned to the fields immediately after giving birth—one form of labor succeeded by another. I imagine the mothers, now and throughout history, who have born

children into wars, refugee camps, brothels, factories, and wildernesses. I think of those who return to work too soon after giving birth—labia swollen, breasts engorged, hearts yearning for their children. Resting in this quiet room, with its lavender walls and view of the forest, I cry with indignation—and also, relief.

7. **Zendo.** I have been meditating for years, but the days and weeks after birth invite me to practice mindfulness in new ways. Being present is suddenly easy: the warmth and weight of you on my naked chest holds my attention for long stretches. Every day demands radical acceptance—of my atrophied limbs, my weak bladder, my sagging cervix; of your wakefulness in the long, gray hours before dawn; of the inert mass of your sleeping father, wrapped in the handmade blanket we received as a wedding gift. And every day demands trust in my ability to feed, soothe, and care for you. I watch you squint at light filtering through leaves, and I see two beginners' minds—yours and my own.

LAND ACKNOWLEDGMENT

Mary Lyons, an elder of the Leech Lake Band of Ojibwe, has said that "Land is part of who we are. It's a mixture of our blood, our past, our current, and our future." Though I don't think I am part of the "we" of whom she spoke, I hope this book testifies to that truth. I also hope it testifies to this truth: that the sacred ground that has been my teacher, companion, and crucible came to me (a White descendant of European colonizers) by way of forced removal, deception, compulsion, broken treaties, and genocide. The beautiful places in this book—and the places from which I wrote these pages—were stolen from their Native inhabitants. Please join me in acknowledging this past, these peoples, and their living descendants.

I wrote and set the opening essay in this collection, "Melt," in Centre County, Pennsylvania, on the traditional territory of the Susquehannock. As early as the seventeenth century, European trade realigned the territories of indigenous nations. In order to monopolize the lucrative fur trade with Europe, the Iroquois pushed southward and westward, effectively destroying the Susquehannock Confederacy. Settlers also invaded the continent and pushed westward, and indigenous peoples in Pennsylvania lost their homes and hunting territories little by little. The Treaty of Paris, which delineated British and American territories at the close of the Revolutionary War in 1783, completely ignored the existence of the continent's Native inhabitants. The following year, representatives from the Iroquois League ceded their nations' claims to the remaining land they controlled in Pennsylvania in the Treaty of Fort Stanwix, which their tribal council refused to ratify and which several other indigenous nations condemned as unjust and invalid. Three Seneca chiefs, in a letter to George Washington in 1790, recounted that treaty in this way:

> When we... heard the invitation which you gave us to draw near to the fire you had kindled and talk with you concerning peace we made haste towards it. You then told us we were in your hand & that by closing it you could crush us to nothing; and you demanded of us a great Country as the price of that peace you had offered us; as if our want of strength had destroyed our rights. Our Chiefs had felt your power & were unable to contend against you and they therefore gave up that Country.

In Centre County, Pennsylvania, I attended graduate school and worked for the Pennsylvania State University—one of fifty-two American Colleges that benefited from the 1862 Morrill Act, which gave states public lands that they could sell or use for profit. Those lands had been taken from their indigenous inhabitants via seizure, unratified treaties, and compelled treaties. Penn State's 780,000-acre land grant included the homelands of more than 112 indigenous nations across the United States, including the Apache, Cheyenne-Arapaho, Ho-Chunk, Klamath, Menominee, Pomo, Sac and Fox Nation, and Yakama. Through the sale of these lands, the University secured $439,000 (about eight million dollars today).

Two of the essays in this collection, "On Naming Women and Mountains" and "Trail Time," are set in national parks in

California's Sierra Nevada. Yosemite National Park and Sequoia and Kings Canyon National Parks are located on the traditional territories of the Ahwahneechee, Miwuk, Paiute, Monache, Nüümü, Western Mono Waksachi, and Yokut peoples. "On Naming Women and Mountains" offers a small glimpse into what happened to this region's indigenous people, but that story is part of a much bigger one. The Mariposa Battalion was just one of many federally funded state militias that began removing indigenous communities from their homelands soon after California achieved statehood in 1850. At least 9,500 Native Americans were murdered in these conflicts in that state alone. Between 1851 and 1892, through a series of treaties, the U.S. Government forced California's tribes to relinquish their rights to their land and relocate to reservations. The people living in what are now Yosemite and Sequoia and Kings Canyon National Parks were removed by Cessions 274 (March 1851) and 279 (May 1851), respectively. California representatives pressured the U.S. Congress not to ratify any of these eighteen treaties so that they would not have to honor them, and they remained secret until 1896. Despite these removal efforts, some Native people remained in the Yosemite region and even lived in the national park, which was established in 1890. In 1906, for unknown reasons, the U.S. Army burned the community residence where the Native Americans in the park lived. Park officials created a new "Indian Village" for Native inhabitants in the 1930s, requiring them to pay rent and submit to Park control. By the early 1950s, only Native Americans employed by the Park and their families were allowed to remain. In 1969, the Park forced the few remaining Native Americans to move into official employee housing and destroyed their village in a practice session for Yosemite firefighters. Starting in the late 1970s, some of the park's Miwuk employees began advocating for the return of their village. It took more than four decades for the Park to agree to allow the local American Indian Council of Mariposa County to rebuild several traditional structures to be used for cultural and religious ceremonies. To this day, the U.S. government does not recognize the legitimacy of the Southern Sierra Miwuk Nation. The Nation is seeking sovereignty rights, which will allow it to govern itself and give it access to health benefits, scholarships, and funding opportunities for federally recognized tribes.

Two of the essays in this collection are set in the Virginias, and several were written or revised from the Shenandoah Valley, where I live and teach for much of the year. "In Between Places" is set in West Virginia's Dolly Sods Wilderness, the traditional territory of the Massawomeck (Iroquois) and also home to Shawnee and Delaware nations at the time of European settlement. "The Weight and Wonder of Everything We Do Not Know" is set in Harrisonburg, Virginia, the traditional territory of the Manahoac and Monacan and later home to the Iroquois. In the 1722 Treaty of Albany between the British and the Haudenosaunee Confederacy (Five Nations of Iroquois), the British agreed that the Blue Ridge Mountains of Virginia would serve as the western boundary of their territory, but White settlers violated the treaty and pushed into the Shenandoah Valley in the 1730s. In 1744, in the Treaty of Lancaster, Virginia negotiators compelled the Haudenosaunee to surrender their land to the "setting sun," which the Iroquois understood as all their territory up to the crest of the Alleghenies (in other words, the Shenandoah Valley). The British, however, used this language to lay claim to all of western Virginia (including the territory that is now Dolly Sods), and some argued that the treaty relinquished to the Crown all the land between Virginia and the Pacific. In the 1752 Treaty of Logstown, the Haudenosaunee Confederacy was forced to surrender its claims to land southeast of the Ohio River. However, other nations, including the Shawnee, still inhabited this territory. The Shawnee vigorously opposed the invasion of White settlers in the Ohio River Valley (which included the territory that later became West Virginia) and in the early 1760s captured all but a few British forts west of the Alleghenies. At this point, England's King George III prohibited settlement west of the Alleghenies in the Proclamation of 1763. However, White settlers again began pouring into the territory when the aforementioned Treaty of Fort Stanwix (1768) ceded the territory between the Ohio River and the Alleghenies to the British. Once again, the Shawnee were inundated by White settlers laying claim to their territory based on a treaty the British negotiated with another indigenous nation. Conflicts between Native Americans and settlers continued in the region into the 1790s, and during that time, frontier settlers formed militias that perpetrated brutal assaults on indigenous communities. In 1794, U.S. troops won a major conflict, the Battle of Timbers, against several allied indigenous nations, including the Shawnee, in northern Ohio. As a result, those nations were forced to cede all territory east and south of Ohio's Cuyahoga River in the Treaty of Greenville, effectively removing all Native American claims to what is now West Virginia.

The essay "Glyphs" is set in western Utah and Eastern Nevada in the traditional territory of the Goshute (Shoshone) people. Given the remoteness and austerity of their territory, the Goshute had few encounters with White people prior to the 1850s, but starting in the 1830s, they were frequent victims of slave raids by neighboring Navajo and Ute peoples, who sold them to Spanish settlers in New Mexico. White Mormons, who believed Utah was a promised land given to them by God, began settling in the Salt Lake Valley in 1847 and soon thereafter began invading Goshute territory. They monopolized desert springs, hunted game, and grazed cattle on fragile meadowland, devastating the Goshutes' hunter-gatherer way of life. Indigenous communities resisted this encroachment, confiscating cattle and horses they found on their land. White settlers often responded to these events with violence. They also chose to route the Pony Express, Overland Stage, and the transcontinental telegraph through Goshute homelands, which created further conflict. Following brutal attacks by both local and federal militias, the Goshute were compelled to enter into a treaty with the U.S. government in 1863. Although they did not cede any land, they agreed to allow Whites to safely pass through their country on several routes, to allow the U.S. military to set up posts, and to permit mining, ranching, and logging on their territory. The federal government agreed to compensate the Goshutes $1,000 a year for twenty years for the destruction of their game. While the Goshute honored their promise of peace, the government began reneging on its treaty obligations before the close of the decade—stopping annual payments and attempting to relocate the Goshute to the reservations of other indigenous nations in Utah, Idaho, Nevada, and Oklahoma. Meanwhile, ranchers and miners continued to use and destroy the natural resources and wildlife on which the Goshute subsisted. In 1912 and 1914, President Taft used executive orders to confine the Goshute to the Skull Valley Reservation (originally just eighty acres) and the Deep Creek Reservation (originally just 34,560 acres). While the reservations have since been expanded to 18,000 and 122,085 acres, respectively, those 218 square miles are a fraction of the territory that once stretched from Utah's Great Salt Lake to Nevada's Steptoe Valley—land the Goshute never ceded.

The essay "Dirty Hands" is set in the Florida Panhandle, in the traditional territory of the Muscogee / Mvskoke (Creek) Nation. The Muscogee descended from a mound-building culture that built elaborate ceremonial complexes and had a sophisticated tribal network throughout the Southeast. By the time the Spanish first arrived on Florida's shores, the Muscogee were a collection of autonomous villages and moderately-sized chiefdoms. Hernando de Soto—whom the King of Spain had appointed "Governor of Cuba"—undertook the first European expedition to inland La Florida in 1539, in search of riches. He and his fellow travelers were likely the first White people the Muscogee encountered. De Soto had been instructed by the King to convert any indigenous people he encountered to Catholicism; instead, he was known for pillaging villages of their food and supplies and enslaving, mutilating, and murdering their inhabitants. Following contact with the Spanish, the Muscogee were ravaged by smallpox and measles epidemics. Then, in the seventeenth and eighteenth centuries, many were enslaved by the British and forced to work on tobacco, rice, indigo, and sugar plantations. During the American Revolution, many in the Creek nations allied with and fought alongside the British, but at the end of the war, the British ceded Muscogee lands to the United States. The new nation's first president, George Washington, developed a six-point plan for "civilizing" the indigenous peoples living in the United States, and he selected the Muscogee to go first. Even before a civil war among the Creeks that thwarted that plan in 1812, U.S. leaders had begun endorsing a policy of "Indian removal." The Muscogee people in Georgia, Alabama, and Florida were compelled to enter eleven treaties between 1790 and 1833 that deprived them of their home-lands. In 1830, President Andrew Jackson signed into law the Indian Removal Act, which forced indigenous people to abandon their homes and relocate to lands west of the Mississippi River. In 1836 and 1837, the U.S. Army forcibly removed more than 20,000 Muscogee people to "Indian Territory" (in present-day Oklahoma) in a campaign of ethnic cleansing that came to be known as The Trail of Tears. In 1898, the U.S. Congress passed the Curtis Act, which abolished tribal governments and forced the break-up of communally held lands of the five major nations in Indian Territory, including the Muscogee (Creek) Nation. Not until 1971 was the Muscogee Nation able to elect a Principal Chief without the approval of the U.S. President. During the forced removal of indigenous Americans during the nineteenth century, some Muscogee escaped from Alabama to the Florida panhandle, where they attempted to reestablish their traditional way of life. They did so at great risk; in addition to federal legislation seeking to banish them, in 1852, Florida's General Assembly passed a law making it unlawful for "any Indian or Indians to remain within the limits of" the state. Those who did remain had to disguise themselves and to carry out any traditional ceremonies or practices in secret. Their descendants, the Muscogee Nation of Florida, have been petitioning for federal acknowledgment since 1978 and continue to be denied recognition, services, and sovereignty by the U.S. government.

The essay "Island, Wilding" is set on Cumberland Island National Seashore, Georgia's southernmost barrier island and the traditional territory of the Tacatacuru (Timucua) people. The Tacatacurus' first known contact with Europeans was in 1562, when their chief met French explorer Jean Ribault's expedition.

After the Spanish established St. Augustine as the capital of La Florida in 1565, they began sending Catholic missionaries northward. In 1587, a priest named Baltazar Lopéz established the San Pedro de Tacatacuru mission on Cumberland Island, where missionaries began converting the Tacatacuru people to Catholicism and a Spanish way of life. Whereas the Tacatacuru had traditionally moved between the island and mainland seasonally, they now began practicing European styles of agriculture and animal husbandry on the island. Over the next century, conflicts between the Spanish and British took a toll on the island's indigenous inhabitants. In 1684, French and English pirate attacks destroyed Cumberland Island's missions. All of the Spanish and many of the Native residents of the island left after those attacks, but some Tacatacuru people remained until James Oglethorpe, founder of the British Colony of Georgia, arrived there in 1736. He built two forts there and forced any remaining Tacatacuru to leave. The Timucua peoples—the broader group to which the Tacatacuru belonged—were decimated not only by these conflicts but by European-borne diseases. Estimated to have numbered about 200,000 at the time of European contact, their numbers had dwindled to 1,000 by 1700 and 167 by 1726. Some Timucua, under Spanish protection, fled to Cuba in 1763. Others are believed to have sought refuge in the Everglades with the Seminoles, and to have traveled with them on the Trail of Tears. The last speakers of the Timucua languages died sometime in the mid-1800s.

A number of essays in this collection—"Cicadas for Lunch," "In the Woods," and "After Birth: The Postpartum Bedroom in Seven Takes"—are set in Coshocton County, Ohio, and much of this book was written in that place. Central Ohio is the traditional territory of the Hopewell, Shawandasse Tula (Shawnee),

Kaskaskia (Illinois), and ꝪΛꝪΛꝪα (Osage) peoples. Many of the indigenous nations residing in the Ohio River Valley at the time of European settlement had ancestral ties to the Hopewell culture (1-400 A.D.)—known for its ceremonial earthworks and beautiful artifacts. Like Pennsylvania's Susquehannock Confederacy, the Osage, Kaskaskia, and Shawnee peoples fought against the Iroquois Confederacy as the fur trade drove it to expand its territory into the Ohio Valley in the seventeenth century. The Osage, who had inhabited the area since 700 B.C., were driven westward as a result of these conflicts. Some Kaskaskia, on the other hand, ended up moving eastward into Ohio after the Treaty of Grande Paix (negotiated between "New France" and forty-nine indigenous nations) brought an end to Iroquois expansion in 1701. In Ohio, as in West Virginia, Shawnee peoples vigorously opposed White settlement in the area. Meanwhile, Native communities that had been forced off lands to the east by White settlers relocated to Ohio. The Lenape (Delaware), displaced by the Treaty of Easton (1758), settled in eastern Ohio and set up their capital in what is now Coshocton County. In 1778, during the American Revolution, three Lenape chiefs signed the Treaty of Fort Pitt. In exchange for the ability of its troops to safely move through Lenape territory, the United States promised to recognize the Lenape as a sovereign nation, guarantee them territorial rights, provide them clothing and weapons, and give them representation in the Continental Congress. This Treaty was never ratified by Congress, and given the nature of its promises, many believe it was signed under false pretenses. Still, in 1781, U.S. Army Colonel Brodhead headed into Lenape territory along the Ohio River with the goal of ensuring that the Native communities had not become loyal to the British. The expedition stopped fifteen miles east of Coshocton and invited several Lenape chiefs to discuss a peaceful resolution to their concerns. They agreed, and as soon as they entered the army encampment, a militiaman killed one of the chiefs with a tomahawk. Broadhead retreated with his men, and fearing retaliation, led a raid on the village of Goschachgunk (now Coshocton). Sixteen Lenape men immediately surrendered, assuming the Americans would honor the Treaty of Fort Pitt, but the militia immediately killed and scalped them. Another twenty Lenape were killed in the ensuing battle, and twenty more (mostly women and children) were taken prisoner. After this event, the remaining Lenape fled to the Sandusky area. In 1796, Coshocton became part of Ohio's United States Military District—2.5 million acres of land grants given to soldiers for their services in the Revolutionary War.

It is important to recognize that Native Americans are not peoples of the past. Neither are attempts to colonize them, to erase them, or to seize their land and resources. It's also important to recognize that North America's indigenous peoples are so much more than the sum of five centuries of brutality and oppression. Their lives and their nations embody resilience, loyalty, creativity, and courage. For these lessons (and so many more) I am forever grateful to Bruce Martin, who invited me to spend three weeks in northern Minnesota as part of his course "Exploring Indigenous Ways of Knowing Among the Anishinaabe" in 2009, and to the Ojibwe of Leech Lake, Red Lake, and White Earth for sharing their land, stories, traditions, history, medicine, and homes with me.

I cannot atone for the past, but I commit to honoring the dead and the living by continuing to educate myself and others about the history of the places I visit and call home; by supporting the work of Native American writers and artists; by advocating for the federal recognition and sovereignty of indigenous nations, the repatriation of Native American remains, and the return of Native American artifacts and ceremonial items; by advocating that the U.S. government honor its treaty obligations to indigenous nations; and by fighting alongside the Water Protectors and other indigenous environmental advocates for the protection of land, water, and wildlife.

ACKNOWLEDGMENTS

John Muir once wrote that "when we try to pick out anything by itself, we find it hitched to everything else in the universe." That's how I feel about this book. It's hitched to every word I've ever read and every mountain I've climbed and every traveler whose path I've crossed somewhere along the way. It would not be were it not for my father, Robert Bryan, who introduced me to the joys of storytelling long before I learned to write. These pages are a testament and tribute to the many fine writing teachers I've had along the way: Harriet Twiggs, Leila Parrish, Bruce Bartholomew, Robert Halback, Marianne Gingher, Sarah Dessen, Lawrence Naumoff, Bland Simpson, Pam Durban, Charlotte Holmes, Bill Cobb, Elizabeth Kadetsky, and Robin Becker. I am also grateful to Bob Burkholder for expanding my exposure to wilderness literature and for introducing me to Dolly Sods Wilderness. Thank you to the many friends and mentors who provided valuable feedback on the essays in this collection, especially Nate Malenke, Patti Malenke, and Natalie Storey.

I am grateful for the staff readers, editors, and contest judges who saw promise in several of the essays that eventually coalesced in this memoir. Judge Julie Marie Wade selected "Melt" as winner of *So to Speak: a feminist journal of language and art's* 2013 Nonfiction Contest; Lee Connel selected "On Naming Women and Mountains" to appear in *Nashville Review* in July 2014; Judith Barrington named "In Between Places" the winner of the 2015 Writers@Work nonfiction contest, which came with publication in *Quarterly West*; Sheryl St. Germain selected "Dirty Hands" for publication in *The Fourth River* in Spring 2016, and Jim Ross republished it in the anthology *In Season: Stories of Discovery, Loss, Home,* and *Places in Between* in 2018; Matthew Shedden selected "The Weight and Wonder of Everything We Do Not Know" to appear in *The Other Journal* in March 2018; Rachel Hartley-Smith selected "In the Woods" to appear in the Spring 2019 issue of *Newfound*; Jimin Han chose "Island, Wilding" as the winner of Parks & Points' Fall 2018 Essay Contest, and Amy Beth Wright published it on that site in Spring 2019; Simmons Buntin selected "After Birth: The Postpartum Bedroom in Seven Takes" to appear on Terrain.org in July 2020; and Juan Morales chose "Trail Time" to appear in *Pilgrimage* in 2022.

Thank you, Leslie M. Browning, for receiving this essay collection with enthusiasm and for offering your discerning eye as an editor. *In Between Places* found the perfect home at Homebound Publications, and I found a community of kindred spirits there.

I am extraordinarily lucky to have a day job that stimulates my mind, lifts my heart, pays the bills, and leaves me with time and energy to write. Thank you to all of the James Madison University colleagues who have supported me in life and work, especially those in the Learning Centers.

The unwavering love and support of my mother, Tina; my siblings, Rachael, Clay, Lee, and Joseph, and their children, Quinn, Stellan, and Blythe; and my chosen family, Patti, Todd, Jael, Kevin, Astrid, Soren, Aaron, Lauren, Carmella, and Oscar have borne me through the trials and triumphs of the last decade. It's also been helpful to have friends who "get me," and I'm especially grateful for my lifelong soul sister, Mary Jane, and my Harrisonburg BFF, Emily.

To those who appear in these pages, thank you for letting me tell my version of our shared stories.

Nate—my husband, my friend, my first reader, my reality check—thank you for being my companion on this journey. I love you. Mads—love of my heart, light of my world—I hope that when you are old enough to read these stories, they will be good company on your own adventures.

ABOUT THE AUTHOR

Lucy Bryan is a writer, adventurer, mother, teacher, and lover of alpenglow, fungi, tiny streams, tall trees, native wildflowers, campfires, homegrown vegetables, thunderstorms, and tents. She splits her time between Ohio's Appalachian Plateau and Virginia's Shenandoah Valley, where she teaches writing at James Madison University. Her award-winning essays have been nominated for the Pushcart Prize and listed as 'notable' in *Best American Essays*. Her nonfiction and fiction have appeared in *Earth Island Journal, Terrain.org, The Other Journal, Superstition Review, Quarterly West,* and *The Fourth River,* among others. She holds a B.A. in journalism from the University of North Carolina at Chapel Hill and an M.F.A. in creative writing from Penn State University. When she's not writing, she enjoys hiking with her kids, cooking with her husband, and napping with her cat.

www.lucybryan.com

HOMEBOUND
PUBLICATIONS

Since 2011 We are an award-winning independent publisher striving to ensure that the mainstream is not the only stream. More than a company, we are a community of writers and readers exploring the larger questions we face as a global village. It is our intention to preserve contemplative storytelling. We publish full-length introspective works of creative non-fiction, literary fiction, and poetry.

Look for Our Imprints Little Bound Books, Owl House Books, The Wayfarer Magazine, Wayfarer Books & Navigator Graphics

WWW.HOMEBOUNDPUBLICATIONS.COM

WAYFARER

BASED IN THE BERKSHIRE MOUNTAINS, MASS.

The Wayfarer Magazine. Since 2012, *The Wayfarer* has been offering literature, interviews, and art with the intention to inspires our readers, enrich their lives, and highlight the power for agency and change-making that each individual holds. By our definition, a wayfarer is one whose inner-compass is ever-oriented to truth, wisdom, healing, and beauty in their own wandering. *The Wayfarer's* mission as a publication is to foster a community of contemplative voices and provide readers with resources and perspectives that support them in their own journey.

Wayfarer Books is our newest imprint! After nearly 10 years in print, *The Wayfarer Magazine* is branching out from our magazine to become a full-fledged publishing house offering full-length works of eco-literature!

Wayfarer Farm & Retreat is our latest endeavor, springing up the Berkshire Mountains of Massachusetts. Set to open to the public in 2024, the 15 acre retreat will offer workshops, farm-to-table dinners, off-grid retreat cabins, and artist residencies.

CPSIA information can be obtained
at www.ICGtesting.com
Printed in the USA
BVHW040530241022
650027BV00002B/141